MENSA
BRAIN
BAFFLERS

Dear Ben,
Reading matter for
the smartest boy
in North Jersey
love
Siz Ryan
Jan '07

MENSA
BRAIN
BAFFLERS

Sterling Publishing Co., Inc.
New York

2 4 6 8 10 9 7 5 3 1

Published in 2006 by Sterling Publishing Co., Inc.
387 Park Avenue South, New York, NY 10016
© 2004 by Sterling Publishing Co., Inc.
Material in this book previously published in *Classic Brain Puzzlers,*
© 1995 by Philip J. Carter & Ken A. Russell,
Take the IQ Challenge, © 1993 by Philip J. Carter & Ken A. Russell
Take the IQ Challenge 3, © 1990 by Philip J. Carter & Ken A. Russell
Distributed in Canada by Sterling Publishing
c/o Canadian Manda Group, 165 Dufferin Street,
Toronto, Ontario, Canada M6K 3H6

Designed by StarGraphics Studio

Sterling ISBN-13: 978-1-4027-4095-4
ISBN-10: 1-4027-4095-6

For information about custom editions, special sales, premium and
corporate purchases, please contact Sterling Special Sales
Department at 800-805-5489 or specialsales@sterlingpub.com.

Contents

CHAPTER TWO
Intelligence Challengers

WHAT IS MENSA?

Mensa The High IQ Society

Mensa is the international society for people with a high IQ. We have more than 100,000 members in over 40 countries worldwide.

Anyone with an IQ score in the top two percent of the population is eligible to become a member of Mensa—are you the "one in 50" we've been looking for?

Mensa membership offers an excellent range of benefits:

- Networking and social activities nationally and around the world;
- Special Interest Groups (hundreds of chances to pursue your hobbies and interests—from art to zoology!);
- Monthly International Journal, national magazines, and regional newsletters;
- Local meetings—from game challenges to food and drink;
- National and international weekend gatherings and conferences;
- Intellectually stimulating lectures and seminars;
- Access to the worldwide SIGHT network for travelers and hosts.

For more information about American Mensa:

www.us.mensa.org
Telephone: (800) 66-MENSA
American Mensa Ltd.
1229 Corporate Drive West
Arlington, TX 76006-6103 USA

For more information about British Mensa (UK and Ireland):

www.mensa.org.uk
Telephone: +44 (0) 1902 772771
E-mail: enquiries@mensa.org.uk
British Mensa Ltd.
St. John's House
St. John's Square
Wolverhampton WV2 4AH
United Kingdom

For more information about Mensa International:

www.mensa.org
Mensa International
15 The Ivories
6–8 Northampton Street
Islington, London N1 2HY
United Kingdom

Introduction

Many Mensa puzzle books rely heavily on the genius of past masters, and this book is no exception. Riddles and puzzles have been propounded from biblical days, when Samson, in Judges XIV:14, asked the Philistines to solve the riddle: 'Out of the eater came forth meat and out of the strong came forth sweetness', right up to modern times with such puzzle masters as Martin Gardner and the 'king of word play,' the late Dmitri Borgmann.

The zenith of puzzle compiling was, we believe, reached during the latter part of the nineteenth century with Lewis Carroll and Sam Lloyd, and was carried on into the first half of the twentieth century by H.E. Dudeney and Hubert Phillips. These four giants of puzzledom were responsible for many new innovations, and we feature several examples of their work throughout this book.

As it draws members from a very wide spectrum of the community, Mensa itself neither expresses nor holds any political or religious views. Indeed, being a round table society with such a diverse membership, it would be impossible for it to do. Members of a like mind are, however, free to group together to form special interest groups devoted to a special interest or opinion, but are not allowed to express opinions as being of Mensa itself.

Should anyone be considering applying for membership, we are sure that, if successful, they will find in Mensa a society which will in some way enrich their lives either through the pages of the excellent Journal, through social contact with other members or through one of the many special interest groups. Indeed, if there is not already a group within Mensa to suit a particular member's needs, he or she is encouraged to start a new group to attract other members of a like mind.

We have tried to include as wide a selection of different types of puzzles as possible, and of varying degrees of difficulty, and we hope there will be something of interest to everyone. The majority of Mensa tests are tests of intelligence rather than of specific general knowledge. Many of the puzzles in this book are purely intelligence problems, but others rely on general knowledge.

The most difficult part of compiling a collection of Mensa Brain Bafflers is what to leave out. Deciding whether one brain-teaser is 'greater' than another has to be subjective, and we have tried to present as varied selection of different types of puzzles as possible, and of varying degrees of difficulty, to give a flavor of the range of puzzles compiled throughout history.

Please enjoy the puzzles, but do not be in too much of a hurry to look at the answers. If you use your imagination, do not always look for the obvious, and put your mind to work, we think you will be able to come up with many of the right answers, but above all we hope you will find the book an interesting and entertaining diversion.

We hope you will regard it as an entertaining, but at the same time serious and important, collection, which will be part of the process of passing such classic puzzles down from one generation to another.

BRAIN
PUZZLERS

PUZZLES ARE FUN

"A quiz should serve to give pleasure to those who take part in it: it is not an examination."

The above was written by Hubert Phillips in June, 1947 as part of the foreword to one of his quiz books published by Ptarmigan Books, called *Who Wrote That?*, and it is exactly our philosophy with respect to both quizzes and puzzles. The late Isaac Asimov once commented that it is extremely dull simply to pick up a book of puzzles and attempt to do them one after the other. We agree that the fun comes from dipping into the book and attempting any puzzle that takes your fancy. The more difficult it is to answer, the more fun it is, especially if you can arrive at the correct answer.

We can think of no better example of a fun puzzle than Sam Loyd's Rick Mules Puzzle, which is, in fact, deceptively difficult. The object is to cut the two dotted lines indicated by the arrow heads and to re-assemble the three resultant pieces so that the two jockeys are riding the mules. The puzzle was sold by Loyd to the American showman P.T. Barnum (of Barnum and Bailey's Circus fame) who sold copies of it at $1 each, and it is said that as a result Loyd earned some $10,000 in royalties.

Sam Loyd was a master at compiling puzzles that appeared so simple to solve that people felt compelled to attempt them, only to find that they would spend hours unsuccessfully trying to figure them out.

You will find other puzzles in the same vein as you dip in and out of this book. Good luck, happy solving and have fun.

P. T. Barnum's
Trick Mules

Cut the card on the dotted lines (into three pieces only) and lay them so that each mule has a correct rider.

Knight's Move

In this book we have included several chess-based problems. This, the first, was devised around 1900 by Boris Kordemsky, the author of *The Moscow Puzzles*.

How can a knight capture all 16 pawns in 16 moves?

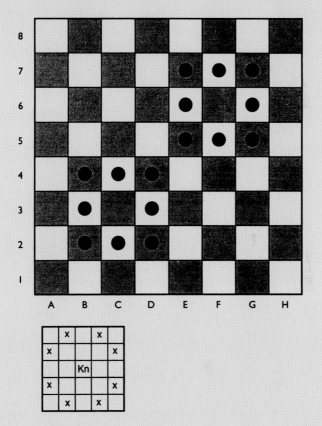

The knight's move in chess

Jigsaw Puzzles

Jigsaw puzzles can be fiendishly difficult, as in the case of this puzzle, which one of the authors recently bought in an antique shop in York.

The puzzle consists of 20 differently shaped pieces, which have to be fitted into the rectangles provided. In the first two puzzles, you are given the first position of some of the pieces and told which numbered pieces are required to cover the rectangle completely. In the third and most difficult puzzle, no pieces have been placed for you.

1. Insert 2, 3, 5, 9, 10, 13, 14, 15, 16 and 18

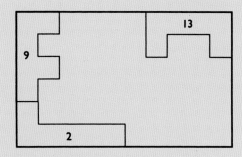

2. Insert 3, 6, 7, 8, 10, 12, 14, 15, 17 and 19

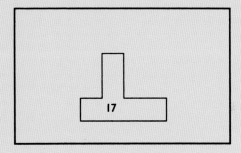

3. Insert 1, 4, 7, 11, 13, 14, 15, 17, 19 and 20

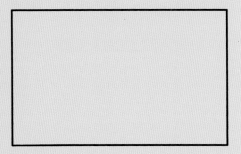

Abracadabra

Abracadabra is a magic word found in amulets. It was featured in a second-century poem by Serenus Sammonicus.

In this puzzle you have to start at the top letter, A, and spell out the word ABRACADABRA by moving downwards. How many different routes are there from top to bottom?

```
                A
              B   B
            R   R   R
          A   A   A   A
        C   C   C   C   C
      A   A   A   A   A   A
    D   D   D   D   D   D   D
  A   A   A   A   A   A   A   A
B   B   B   B   B   B   B   B   B
R   R   R   R   R   R   R   R   R   R
A   A   A   A   A   A   A   A   A   A   A
```

Sam Loyd's
Hoop-Snake Puzzle

This is a great puzzle, which was devised by Sam Loyd. In it he relates the story of Professor Von Schafskoppen, the distinguished naturalist, who scours the country in search of the legendary hoop-snake, which travels around the countryside at great speed by taking the end of its tail in its mouth and rolling along the ground in the shape of a hoop. Eventually the professor finds a petrified hoop-snake, still with its tail in its mouth. To facilitate transportation, he cuts the snake into 10 pieces and returns to his laboratory. Unfortunately, he has since been trying to find how to put the hoop-snake back together again correctly.

Can you arrange the ten pieces so that the snake will bite its tail? After placing the tail correctly in the snake's mouth, there are 40,320 different ways of putting the remaining eight pieces together, but only one of these will produce the desired solution.

King Jovial's Party

The following logic puzzle was compiled by Hubert Phillips for his book *Brush up Your Wits*.

"I've just been staying," writes Toady, "at the court of King Jovial of Hilaria. Everything there is delightfully informal.

"We dined, for instance, at a Round Table (thus avoiding difficult questions of precedence). There were twelve of us at the table—six husbands and their wives—and the rule was that no husband sat next to his wife, but was separated from her by the same number of places. For instance, Queen Cilly sat opposite to Lady Peekaboo, while the Duke of Dull Ness sat three places to the Queen's left. I was three places to the Duchess's right, the Marchioness of Muttonfat was two places from the Queen, while my wife sat opposite Lady Parsley."

Draw a plan of the table showing how the 12 diners were seated.

Schiller's Riddle

Can you solve the following brain teaser? It is by Johann Christoph Friedrich von Schiller (1759-1805), the German dramatist, poet and historian who compiled several riddles, which were contained in *Ilirandot* (1802) and *Parabein und Ratsel* (1803).

For ages an edifice here has been found
   It is not a dwelling it is not a fane;
A horseman for hundreds of days may ride round,
   Yet the end of the journey he ne'er can attain.
Full many a century o'er it has pass'd,
   The might of the storm and of time it defies;
'Neath the rainbow of Heaven stands free to the last,
   In the ocean it dips, and soars up to the skies.
It was not a vain glory bade its erection
   It serves as a refuge, a shield or protection;
Its like on the earth never yet has been known
   And yet by man's hand it is fashion'd alone.

Nine Green Bottles

A wine merchant had a dishonest employee who regularly helped himself to bottles of wine. Eventually the merchant decided to catch the employee. He had 28 green bottles of wine in his store and arranged them as shown in the diagram so that there were nine bottles along each side. The employee, however, realized that the trap had been set, so when he took away four bottles he rearranged the remainder so that there were still nine bottles along each side. Later he returned and took four more bottles and again rearranged the remainder so that there were nine bottles on each side. How did he do this?

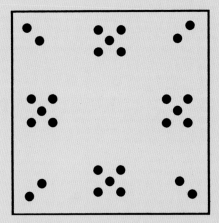

A Revolutionary Tale

A rebus is an arrangement of pictures, letters or symbols to suggest a word, name or phrase. They were fashionable around 100 years ago and have recently become very popular again. This one was collected by Sam Loyd. What does it represent?

Married Couples

This simple little puzzle is based on a logic puzzle known to be at least 60 years old.

A man leaves $10,000 in his will, to which there are six separate beneficiaries—his three sons and their wives. The three wives in total receive $3,960, of which Janice gets $100 more than Susan and Helen gets £100 more than Janice. Of the sons, James gets twice as much as his wife, Alec gets the same as his wife and Peter gets 50 per cent more than his wife. Who is married to whom?

COMPLEXITIES

The common feature shared by all the puzzles in this section is that they involve complex solutions. They are not the type of puzzle you can solve in an instant, and it is necessary to sit down with a pencil and paper and work your way through each puzzle stage by stage in a logical manner to arrive at a structured solution. They are the type of puzzle in which your time and patience are rewarded with a great deal of satisfaction when eventually you arrive at a correct solution—a philosphy that is reinforced in one of the author's 1986 puzzles, reproduced here as Word Square.

Word Square

Begin at the top left-hand corner and travel to the bottom right-hand corner by moving from letter to letter, vertically, horizontally or diagonally, to unscramble a hidden message. You have to visit each square once only, and there are no redundant squares.

W	E	S	I	H	B	E	Y	D	D
C	H	S	F	S	T	D	O	N	O
C	U	E	P	U	E	E	T	B	U
S	N	L	L	U	V	T	I	Q	A
U	Y	Y	Z	O	E	T	I	L	U
C	O	Z	R	L	S	E	N	A	N
Y	O	L	P	P	O	I	O	P	D
O	E	M	E	F	A	T	A	T	I
W	U	L	V	D	N	I	R	N	E
I	L	H	A	E	T	E	M	C	E

Mr. Etcher

The following logic puzzle was devised by Hubert Phillips.

Messrs. Draftsman, Etcher, Musician and Sculptor are a draftsman, an etcher, a musician and a sculptor. Of none, however, are the name and vocation the same. The draftsman is not the namesake of Mr. Musician's vocation. The etcher is neither Mr. Sculptor, nor the namesake of Mr. Etcher's vocation.

Can you say what Mr. Etcher's vocation is?

The Spider and the Fly

This puzzle was devised by H. E. Dudeney.

Inside a rectangular room, which is 30 feet long and 12 feet wide and high, a spider is at a point in the middle of one of the end walls, 1 foot from the ceiling, at point A, and a fly is on the opposite wall, 1 foot from the floor in the center, at point B.

What is the shortest distance that the spider may crawl in order to reach the fly, which remains stationary?

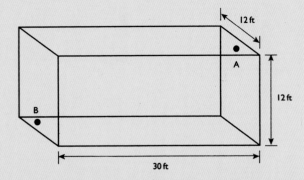

How to Make a Chinese Cross

This puzzle was sent to one of the authors several years ago by Doug Pattinson, a Mensa member from Leeds, UK. It was dated 1881 and had been handed down through Mr. Pattinson's family. Just to prove it worked in practice, Mr. Pattinson constructed the puzzle in wood as a gift for the author. See if you can work out the answer using a pencil and paper. Alternatively, the craftspeople among you may try to emulate Mr. Pattinson by constructing the puzzle yourselves. The instructions given here are as they were originally written.

Having six pieces of wood, bone, or metal, made of the same length as in No. 6 in the figures below, and each piece of the same size as No. 7 it is required to construct a cross, with six arms, from these pieces, in such a manner that it shall not be displaced when thrown upon the floor.

The shaded part of each figure represents the parts that are cut out of the wood, and each piece marked "a" is supposed to be facing the reader, while the pieces marked 1' are the right side of each piece turned over towards the left, so as to face the reader. No. 7 represents the end of each piece of wood, and is given to show the dimensions.

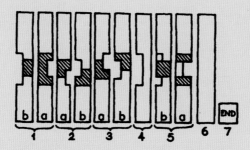

Probability

It was not until the seventeenth century, when the French mathematician Blaise Pascal formulated the first rules relating to probability, that people were really aware that such laws existed. Until then, gambling had been governed by gut feeling and comparison of results.

Here is a typical example of a puzzle based on the rules of probability. A total of 20 white balls and 30 black balls are placed in a box. What are the chances of drawing out in turn:

1. Black then white?

2. White then black?

3. White followed by white?

4. Black followed by black?

The above should be treated as four separate puzzles, i.e., in puzzle 1 the black ball is drawn out and remains out and then the white ball is drawn out. All the balls are back in the bag for puzzle 2.

The Golf Club Statistician

This puzzle was compiled by one of the authors in 1986.

I won all three major knockout competitions at my golf club last year (wishful thinking), even though I was the only player unlucky enough to be drawn in both preliminary rounds.

Recently, our dub statistician stopped me and said, "Do you know, I cubed the number of entrants for each competition, and the last digit of each of the three resultant numbers is the same as your golf handicap, and the sum of the three middle digits (i.e., the middle digit of each of the cube numbers) is the same as mine; also, the total number of rounds you have won is the same as your wife's handicap, which is exactly double your own handicap. Furthermore, the total number of matches played, including the end-of-season consolation event for players knocked out in the preliminary rounds, is the same as the age of Seth Arkwright, our surviving founder member."

What are mine, my wife's and the dub statistician's handicaps, and how old is Seth Arkwright?

Couriers

This puzzle is taken from the *Treviso Arithmetic* (1478).

The Holy Father sent a courier from Rome to Venice to reach Venice in 7 days. The Signoria of Venice sent a courier to Rome to reach Rome in 9 days. The distance was 250 miles.

In how many days will they meet?

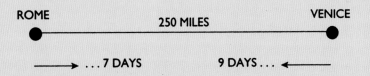

Excelsior

In 1885 Lewis Carroll published a series of puzzles under the general heading *A Tangled Tale*, which was divided into 10 chapters called 'knots'. The puzzles were incorporated into a narrative and each knot had to be untangled by readers, with whom he built up a lively correspondence. The following puzzle, which appeared in Knot One, is entitled Excelsior.

Two travellers spend from 3 o'clock till 9 o'clock in walking along a level road, up a hill, and home again; their pace on the level being 4 miles an hour, up hill 3, and down hill 6. Find the distance walked: also (within half an hour) the time of reaching the top of the hill.

The Engine Driver

Here is another puzzle, dating from around 1900, by Boris Kordemsky, author of *The Moscow Puzzles*.

On the Moscow-Leningrad train are three passengers named Ivanov, Petrov, and Sidorov. By coincidence, the engine driver, the fireman, and the guard have the same three last names.

1. Passenger Ivanov lives in Moscow.

2. The guard lives halfway between Moscow and Leningrad.

3. The passenger with the same name as the guard lives in Leningrad.

4. The passenger who lives nearest the guard earns exactly three times as much per month as the guard.

5. Passenger Petrov earns 200 roubles a month.

6. Sidorov (a member of the crew) recently beat the fireman at billiards.

What is the engine driver's last name?

Much Giggling

The following puzzle was compiled by Hubert Phillips and was published in his book *Brush up Your Wits*.

The old market town of Much Giggling has a town council of nine members. These are Messrs. Baker, Butcher, Brewer, Carter, Draper, Ironmonger, Painter, Saddler and Smith. These gentlemen are (not necessarily respectively) a baker, a butcher, a brewer, a carter, a draper, an ironmonger, a painter, a saddler and a smith.

The saddler is the ironmonger's father-in-law. Mr. Saddler is engaged to the painter's only daughter, who has already rejected Mr. Saddler's rivals, the draper and the baker. Mr. Carter's daughter partners her fiancé at tennis. Mr. Draper, who is a bachelor, has succeeded the namesake of his vocation as captain of the cricket team. Mr. Smith shares an allotment with his son-in-law. The draper's father is a brother of the wife of Mr. Baker. The brewer and the carter are married to each other's sisters. No councillor has more than one daughter; two councillors have one each. The brewer is the namesake of the vocation of the namesake of the vocation of Mr. Carter, and the carter is the namesake of the vocation of the namesake of the vocation of Mr. Smith.

Identify the vocation of each of the nine councillors.

The Ultimate Shunting Puzzle

This puzzle was sent to us by a Mensa member several years ago. Unfortunately, he did not know its source, but it is one of the best of its kind we have seen, so it's hats off to the compiler, whoever he or she may be.

The train is 10 meters long, and the coaches are each 5 meters long. All other dimensions, apart from those shown, can be any length. By shunting you have to reverse the positions of coach A and coach B and return the train to its starting point.

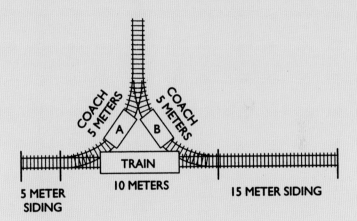

Cross-Numbers

This cross-number was devised by H. E. Dudeney.

Across

1 A square number
4 A square number
5 A square number
8 The digits sum to 35
11 Square root of 30 across
13 A square number
14 A square number
15 Square of 36 across
17 Square of half 11 across
18 Three similar figures
19 Product of 4 across and 33 across
21 A square number
22 5 times 5 across
23 All digits alike except the central one
25 Square of 2 down
27 See 20 down
28 A fourth power
29 Sum of 18+31 across
31 A triangular number
33 1 more than 4 times 36 across
34 Digits sum to 18 and the 3 middle numbers are 3
36 An odd number
37 All digits even except one, and their sum is 29
39 A fourth power
40 A cube power
41 Thrice a square

Down

1 Reads both ways alike
2 Square root of 28 across
3 Sum of 17 across +21 across
4 Digits sum to 19
5 Digits sum to 26
6 Sum of 14+33 across
7 A cube number
9 A cube number
10 A square number
12 Digits sum to 30
14 All similar figures
16 Sum of digits is 12 down
18 All similar digits excepting first
20 Sum of 17+27 across
21 Multiple of 19
22 A square number
24 A square number
26 Square of 18 across
28 A fourth power of 4 across
29 Twice 15 across
30 A triangular number
32 Digits sum to 20
34 6 times 21 across
35 A cube number
37 A square number
38 A cube number

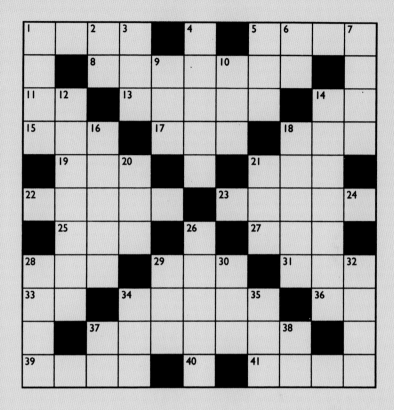

Joyville

Here is another puzzle that was included by Hubert Phillips in his book *Brush up Your Wits*.

I have had a number of letters from some young friends of mine, in which they all refer to a sort of beauty competition they have all been in.

From Basil: I've been acting as one of the judges to choose Miss Joyville. Six girls competed, and it was agreed that each of the ten judges should have ten votes to distribute as he

continued

liked among the competitors, but that as a safeguard against "plumping" none of us would give a "duck" to more than one competitor. Annette was undoubtedly the winner–at any rate eight of us thought so. But the judging was a puzzling business, and in my view there was nothing to choose between the rest of the competitors.

From Hamish: I didn't quite agree with Basil; I thought that Fern was every bit as attractive as Annette, but I did agree with him about the rest, and Victor thought that some other girl shared Annette's pedestal.

From Fern: Annette got four times as many votes as I did; three of the judges gave me no votes at all, and Jim, my fiancé, only bracketed me second with Sofia; even so, she did better than I did, though she got no votes at all from either Alec or Stephen and only one from Lionel.

From Mayblossom: I only got third place. Teddy–the blighter–gave me no marks at all, and even Victor gave Annette one more than me.

From Everard: Annette was an easy winner. I thought her worth more than all the others put together, and Lionel was nearly as enthusiastic. But no two of us distributed his votes numerically in exactly the same way. Geoffrey had the strange idea of giving Sofia second place; in actual fact the second place went to Helen.

From Prudence: I was rather a flop, but anyway Alec thought me just as good as Mayblossom, and better than Helen, and I'm bucked at beating Sonia.

Now, just how did those 10 judges distribute their votes?

THE OLD FAVORITES

The authors can recall many puzzles that they heard of as children. For example, in the Frog in the Circle the question is posed: "How many jumps is a frog required to make to get out of a circle if it starts in the center, jumps half the radius with its first leap, then half the distance remaining, then half again, and so on?" The answer, of course, is that it never will escape from the circle no matter how agonizingly close to the circumference it reaches. A similar paradox was posed by the ancient Greek Zeno, around 450 B.C., in which he proposes that in a race between Achilles and the Tortoise, if Achilles gives the tortoise a start he cannot overtake it, for whenever he arrives where the tortoise was, it has already moved on.

There are scores of other old favorite classic puzzles, many of which have their origins deep in history and of which we present a small selection in this section.

The Bookworm

In my library is a three-volume encyclopedia. Taking it from the shelf one day, I was annoyed to see that a bookworm had eaten its way in a straight line from the first page of volume 1 to the last page of volume 3. I measured the thickness of the books and found that each was 2¼ inches across, the pages being 2 inches thick and the covers ⅛ inch each.

How far had the bookworm travelled?

The Famous Farmer's Horses Puzzle

A long time ago a farmer died and left 19 horses to be divided among his three sons. The eldest son was to inherit half, the next son was to have a quarter and the youngest son a fifth. However, the will stated that none of the horses was to be slaughtered to help in the division. While they were pondering how it was to be possible to divide 19 by 2, 4 or 5 parts without a remainder, a neighboring farmer rode up, jumped off his horse and put it with the 19, making 20. Then he gave half (10) to the eldest brother, a quarter (5) to the second brother and a fifth (4) to the youngest brother. The 10, 5 and 4 horses made 19, the twentieth horse was returned to the neighboring farmer, and he departed, having done his good deed for the day. The brothers were all happy with this but were never able to understand why.

What is the explanation? Why was it possible for the neighbor to add his own horse to the others, do the dividing exactly as required by the will and have his own horse returned to him at the end?

The Slug in the Well

A slug is at the bottom of a well and decides to make his way to the top. He climbs up 3 feet each day, but then slips back 2 feet during his night-time slumber. The well is 20 feet deep. How long does it take the slug to get to the top?

The Broken Clock Face

This clock was dropped on the floor and the face broke into four pieces. When the bits were picked up it was noticed that the numbers on all four pieces added up to the same amount. What was the amount and what did each piece contain?

The Water Butt

Two farm laborers were arguing about a water butt. One said it was less than half full and the other said it was more than half full. To settle the argument they asked the farmer to adjudicate. Although there were no other implements or vessels at hand with which to measure the water the farmer was quickly able to determine who was correct. How did he do it?

The Capital and Labor Puzzle

The puzzle illustrated is a reproduction of a river-crossing puzzle devised in 1910.

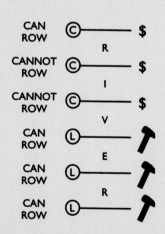

Three laborers and three capitalists must cross a river. However, as the laborers do not trust the capitalists, they (the capitalists) cannot at any time outnumber the laborers on either side of the river. How do the six achieve the crossing as efficiently as possible—i.e., in the fewest possible number of moves—given that the boat holds only two people and, although all the laborers can row, only one of the capitalists can row?

The Wolf, Goat and Cabbage

This puzzle dates from the eighth century.

A man has to take a wolf, a goat and a cabbage across a river. His rowboat can take:

Man plus wolf, or man plus goat, or man plus cabbage.

If he takes the cabbage, the wolf will eat the goat. If he takes the wolf, the goat will eat the cabbage. How does he get the three across?

The Jealous Husbands

This river-crossing puzzle was compiled by Claude-Jasper Batchet in 1612.

Three jealous husbands with their wives have to cross a river by rowboat. The boat can carry only two persons at a time. Only three people out of the six can row. How can the six people cross the river so that none of the women shall be left in the company of any of the men, unless when her husband is present?

The Ant on
the Elastic Band

A 3-inch long elastic band is fixed at one end. An ant crawls along it at the rate of 1 inch per minute. After 1 minute the band is stretched by 3 inches. The ant then crawls along at the same rate and after 1 minute the band is stretched a further 3 inches. This cycle continues at the end of each minute, until the ant reaches the end of the band. Assuming that the band is capable of being stretched so far, how long will it take the ant to reach the end?

VISUAL PUZZLES

Probably the first visual puzzles we can all remember from childhood are the visual deception puzzles, of which we present several examples in this section, including Circles. There are, however, many other types of visual puzzle–matchstick puzzles, as in Matchsticks, counting triangles, of which the one shown in Triangles 1 was composed by one of the the authors in 1986; and mazes, such as the one shown here, which is taken from a book of designs for garden mazes, *Architectura Curiosa* by G. A. Boeckler, which was published in 1664.

Circles

Which is the larger circle, A or B?

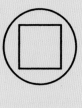 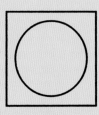

A   B

Matchsticks

Add five matches to make nine.

Triangles 1

How many triangles are there in this figure?

Jumping Coins

Twelve coins are arranged in the same positions as numbers on the face of a clock. Pick up any coin and jump over two coins in any direction–clockwise or counterclockwise–and place it on the third coin. In six such moves, form six stacks of two coins each.

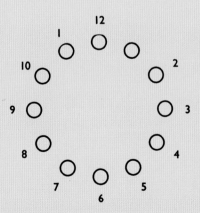

Rebuses 1

A rebus is an arrangement of letters that indicate a word or phrase–for example, BBBBBB = bee line. The first of the 18 examples below is a classic rebus, many years old, and the answer that you are looking for is a quotation from Shakespeare. The remaining 17 were compiled by the authors between 1984 and 1993, and they may be a one-word answer or a well-known phrase or saying.

1	2	3
KIND	I I I I I I I I I I S S S S S S S S S S	i i i i i i I
4	**5**	**6**
TOCCDUN	MEAS	RACT
7	**8**	**9**
NEMT	HYDE HYDE	BIBLE
10	**11**	**12**
R I A N B	TUASPRF	AS TAT EOF
13	**14**	**15**
JOL [2♦] SON	THE FIFTH	: : C
16	**17**	**18**
LIS	AALLLL	GNINWOD

Nine Trees 1

The following puzzle is attributed to Sir Isaac Newton, and appeared in the book *Rational Amusement for Winter Evenings* by John Jackson, which was published in 1821.

The object of the puzzle is to plant nine trees so that they form ten straight rows with three trees in every row.

● ● ●

● ● ●

● ● ●

Visual Deceptions

There are many puzzles designed to deceive the eye. These three are typical examples, and you have to solve each one using the naked eye only.

1. Which of the two horizontal lines is longer?

2. These two strips were cut from a circle. Which is the longer piece?

A   B

3. In which of the figures, A or B, is the vertical line longer?

A   B

Hooves

This dissection puzzle is by H. E. Dudeney. Each hoof has to be cut into two pieces and the four resultant pieces re-assembled to form a circle.

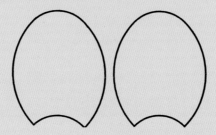

The 36-Coin Puzzle

Take away six coins so that all the rows that are left contain an even number, whether reckoned vertically, horizontally or corner-to-corner.

Triangles 2

Arrange the six matches to form four triangles.

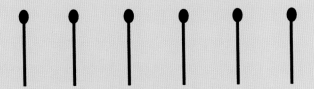

Squaring the Urn

This puzzle dates back to the Ancient Egyptians.

Draw two straight lines to cut the shaded section into three pieces that can be arranged to form a square.

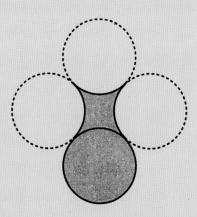

The Classic
Letter H Puzzle

There are a number of dissection puzzles involving letters. This example and The Triangular H involve assembling the letter H.

This puzzle was produced in the 1920s, and it is an adaptation of the classic letter T puzzle, with which many of you will be familiar. The object is to arrange the six pieces to form a letter H. It is a deceptively difficult puzzle.

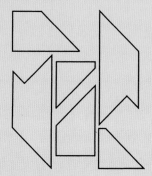

The Triangular H

This puzzle was produced by N. K. Atlas of Paris in 1920. It calls for a certain amount of ingenuity on the part of the solver.

Can you arrange the eight triangular pieces into the shape of a letter H?

31 Lines

This is a good example of a puzzle in which you have to draw around a figure without lifting your pencil from the paper and without going over any part twice. This particular puzzle is known to be at least 60 years old.

Can you negotiate the 31 lines in the correct order?

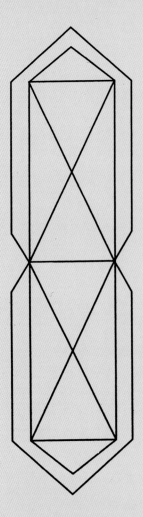

CLASSIC MATHEMATICAL PUZZLES

It would not be possible to include every classic mathematical puzzle ever compiled in just one book, and at best all we can attempt to do is present a carefully chosen, typical and challenging selection.

In any book of classic puzzles the name Sam Loyd is always going to be at the forefront, and, as you will have already gathered, this book is no exception. He was responsible for many classic mathematical puzzles, of which one of the most famous is illustrated here, which he invented in the 1870s and called the 14-15 Puzzle in Puzzleland. It was to lead to the invention of many other sliding-block puzzles with which many of you will be familiar. The puzzle consisted of a square base in which 15 blocks were arranged in regular order, but with the 14 and 15 reversed. The object was to move the blocks about, one at a time, and to return them to their present positions, except that the error in the positions of 14 and 15 was corrected. In the words of Loyd, the puzzle "drove the entire world crazy," and he offered a prize of $1,000 for the first correct solution.

1	2	3	4
5	6	7	8
9	10	11	12
13	15	14	

The money was never claimed, however, because, as Loyd already knew, there was no possible solution. He had realized that half the possible starting positions do not lead to a solution because rearrangement of the blocks by sliding them only gives rise to an equal number of exchanges. He changed the position of 14 and 15 and challenged the solver to correct their positions but, since this is equivalent to only a single, uneven exchange of blocks, it was impossible. The mathematics of the puzzle is that there are over 600 billion arrangements of the blocks that can be made from the original position and there is an equal number that cannot be made. As Loyd himself put it: "The original problem is impossible to solve except by such skulduggery as turning the 6 and 9 blocks upside down. One of the puzzle's peculiarities is that any such interchange involving two blocks immediately converts the puzzle to a solvable one. In fact, any odd number of interchanges has the same effect, whereas an even number leaves the puzzle unsolvable as before."

On this occasion, however, Loyd did not have the last laugh. There was an amusing twist in the tale when Loyd applied to patent the puzzle. In those days it was necessary to present a working model of a device, but when the Patent Commissioner was told that no solution existed he retorted: "Then you can't have a patent. If the thing won't work, how can you file a working model of it!"

The Laborer's Puzzle

Here is another puzzle by H. E. Dudeney.

During one of his rambles, Professor Rackbrane chanced to come upon a man digging a deep hole.

"Good morning" he said. "How deep is that hole?"

"Guess" replied the laborer. "My height is exactly 5 feet 10 inches."

"How much deeper are you going?" asked the Professor.

"I am going twice as deep," was the answer, "and then my head will be twice as far below ground as it is now above ground."

Rackbrane now asks if you could tell how deep that hole would be when it was finished.

Carpenter

The following puzzle is the work of Nicolas Chuquet, a French mathematician who wrote *Triparty en la science des nombres* in 1484.

A carpenter agrees to work on the condition that he is paid 2 units for every day that he works, while he forfeits 3 units for every day that he does not work.

At the end of 30 days he finds that he has paid out exactly as much as he has received. How many days did he work?

The Soldier's Return

This is one of Lewis Carroll's best known brain teasers.

On return from the battlefield, the regiment is badly battle-scarred. If 70 percent of the soldiers have lost an eye, 75 percent have lost an ear, 85 percent have lost a leg and 80 percent have lost an arm, what percentage at least must have lost all four?

The Diophantine Squares

Diophantus was a third century A.D. Greek mathematician who lived at Alexandria. Of his three known works, only six books of his treatise on algebra, *Arithmetica*, have survived. The following puzzle is one of the earliest problems in mathematics, and was one of several solved by Diophantus.

Find three numbers such that their sum is a perfect square, and the sum of any two is perfect square.

Can you find the three numbers, all of which are less than 500?

How Old Is Mary?

H. E. Dudeney included this puzzle in one of his books in 1917 and described it as "a funny little age problem, by the late Sam Loyd, which has been very popular in the United States."

The combined ages of Mary and Ann are 44 years, and Mary is twice as old as Ann was when Mary was half as old as Ann will be when Ann is three times as old as Mary was when Mary was three times as old as Ann. How old is Mary? That is all, but can you work it out?

Houses

A. Henry Rhind, a Scottish Egyptologist purchased the "Rhind Papyrus", a rich source of the work of Egyptian mathematicians. The papyrus, which is 18 feet 6 inches long and 13 inches wide, dates from 1650 BC. The writing covers both sides and includes the following puzzle.

There are seven houses each containing seven cats. Each cats kill seven mice, and each mouse would have eaten seven ears of spelt. Each ear of spelt would have produced seven hekats of grain. What is the total of all these?

Dishes

This ancient Chinese puzzle, which dates from the fourth century A.D., is by Sun Tsu Suan-Ching.

"How many guests are there?" said the official.

"I do not know," said the cook, "but every two used a dish for rice between them, every three used a dish for broth between them and every four used a dish for meat between them."

There were 65 dishes in all. How many guests were there?

Coins

The Bhakshali Manuscript was found in 1881 in northwest India and dates from the third to the twelfth centuries. In it is the following puzzle.

Twenty men, women and children earn 20 coins between them.

Each man earns 3 coins

Each woman earns $1^1/_2$ coins

Each child earns $^1/_2$ coin

How many men, women and children are there?

Alphametics

Puzzles in which numbers were replaced by letters first appeared thousands of years ago in Ancient China. Originally they were known as letter arithmetics, then cryptarithms and, since 1955, alphametics.

1. In the division sum below each letter stands for a different number. None of the digits in the divisor (135) occurs elsewhere in the sum, and there is no remainder. Can you complete the sum?

```
1 3 5 ) P H I L ( P P
        P I L
        ─────
        P I L
        P I L
        ─────
```

2. Here is another division sum, but this is more difficult.

```
M Y ) W O R D ( K E N
      N W
      ─────
        G R
        Y R
        ─────
        M D D
          R M
        ─────
            R
```

The Collector's Bequest

If you know a unique fact about a certain number it should be possible to construct a puzzle from it. This is one such puzzle, which was compiled by one of the authors in 1989.

A rich collector of gold coins left a very complicated will giving instructions about how his gold coin collection (of fewer than 5,000 coins) was to be distributed among his ten children–five sons and five daughters–after his death. The instructions he gave were that first of all one gold coin was to be given to his butler, then exactly a fifth of those remaining had to go to his eldest son. Another coin was then given to the butler, then exactly a fifth of those still remaining went to his next eldest son. This procedure was repeated exactly until all his five sons had received a share, and the butler had been given five gold coins. Then, after the fifth son had taken his share the gold coins still remaining were to be equally divided among his five daughters. How many gold coins did the collector have in his collection?

Catching a Thief

"Now Constable," said the defendant's counsel in cross-examination. "You say that the prisoner was exactly 27 steps ahead of you when you started to run after him?"

"Yes, sir."

"And you swear that he takes eight steps to your five?"

"That is so."

"Then I ask you, Constable, as an intelligent man, to explain how you ever caught him if that is the case?"

"Well you see sir, I have got a longer stride. In fact, two of my steps are equal in length to five of the prisoner's. If you work it out, you will find that the number of steps I required would bring me exactly to the spot where I captured him."

Here the foreman of the jury asked for a few minutes to work out the number of steps the constable must have taken. Can you also say how many steps the officer needed to catch the thief?

2520

This is another puzzle devised by Boris Kordemsky in about 1900.

Scholars discovered "2520" in hieroglyphics engraved on a stone lid of a tomb in an Egyptian pyramid. Why was such an honor paid to this number?

The Average Speed Paradox

A car travels at a speed of 20 mph over a certain distance and then returns over the same distance at a speed of 30 mph. What is the average speed for the total journey?

Napoleon's Problem

This puzzle is believed to have been proposed to Napoleon by the mathematician Loren Mascheroni, who was famous for his constructions.

1. Divide a circle with a known centre into four equal arcs using only a pair of compasses.

2. Rider: prove it.

The solution you are seeking was included by H. E. Dudeney in his 1926 book *Modern Puzzles.*

Filling a Bath

Bath puzzles appear in many forms, but this is a typical example.

You have accidentally left out the plug and are attempting to fill the bath with both taps full on. The hot tap takes 6 minutes to fill the bath, the cold tap takes 4 minutes, and the water empties through the plug hole in 12 minutes. In how many minutes will the bath be filled?

Magic Squares 1

Magic squares are of great interest to us and we have a large collection of them. They were developed by the Ancient Chinese and consist of an array of numbers in which all rows, columns and diagonals add up to the same total. Here are five examples, each getting progressively more difficult.

1. This square is known as the Lo-shu, and, according to Chinese legend, it is the first ever magic square. It is said to have appeared to the mythical Emperor Yu on the back of a tortoise. Your task is to re-create the square by inserting the numbers from 1 to 9 once each only so that each row, column and corner-to-corner diagonal adds up to 15. There is only one possible way in which this can be done, not counting rotations and reflections.

2. Insert the remaining numbers from 1 to 16 so that each row, column and corner-to-corner line adds up to 34.

16			
			8
		12	
			4

3. Insert the remaining numbers from 1 to 25 so that each row, column and corner-to-corner line adds up to 65.

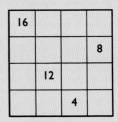

4. Insert the remaining numbers from 1 to 36 so that each row, column and corner-to-corner line adds up to 111.

24			6		
		12			30
	18			36	

5. This is three magic squares in one. Insert the remaining numbers from 1 to 49 so that each row, column and corner-to-corner line adds up to 175. In addition, the middle 3 x 3 square will add up to 75, and the inner 5 x 5 square will add up to 125!

					49	
					35	
		21			14	7
		28				
		42				

WORD PLAY

Word puzzles are probably the most popular and widely published of all puzzles, whether they be crosswords, anagrams, cryptograms or acrostics. Words are something with which everyone is familiar, for we all have to understand and speak the language to communicate, and the challenge of solving a word puzzle is one to which most of us like to respond.

We enjoy compiling puzzles as much as we enjoy solving them, and to try to illustrate our point we are presenting the following experiment, which we will call "reverse anagrams" in which we invite you to be the compiler. We are listing a number of words, names or phrases and challenge you to come up with an appropriate anagram for each.

TELEVISION NEWS
FLORENCE NIGHTINGALE
GROVER CLEVELAND
LITTLE RED RIDING HOOD
LIKE A LAMB TO THE SLAUGHTER
PRESBYTERIAN
GOLDEN WEDDINGS
THE GOOD SAMARITANS
THE TOWERING INFERNO

When you think you have exhausted all the possibilities turn to Word Play Introduction of Brain Puzzlers, where you will find one anagram for each of the above, together with the name of the compiler, where known. How many of you, we wonder, found the same anagram or something even more appropriate?

The Hyperion Diamond

Crossword puzzles evolved from nineteenth-century puzzles called word forms, in which words are interlocked in geometric shapes. The first form published in America was a square, and appeared in a sporting paper *Wilkes' Spirit of the Times*, on 24 September 1859.

```
C I R C L E
I C A R U S
R A R E S T
C R E A T E
L U S T R E
E S T E E M
```

By the 1870s some puzzle constructors were producing what were termed double forms, in which different words read across and down. The following is in the shape of a diamond, and it was compiled by someone using the pseudonym Hyperion in *St Nicholas Magazine* of September, 1875.

We have filled in the vowels, and you have to add the consonants to form words both across and down.

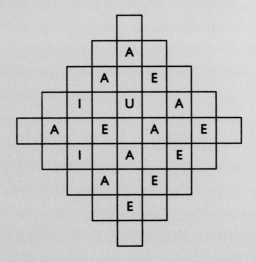

Curiosity in Words

Here is a curiosity dating from the First World War when the names
listed below were on everybody's lips.

There is nothing particularly unusual about the names
though–or is there?

KAISER
SERBIA
JOFFRE
FRENCH

Beheadments

This riddle is taken from Sam Loyd's *Cyclopedia of Puzzles*, which was
published in 1914.

In yon vast field of cultivated space,
I there am found with members of my race;
Decapitate me—if you've no objection—
You then will find what brings me to perfection;
Take one more cut, and then you'll plainly see,
What I am destined, day by day, to be.

Double-Cross Alphabet

This puzzle was compiled by the authors in 1987. We have compiled 160 cross-alphabet puzzles in which the object is to use each of the 26 letters of the alphabet once each only to form a crossword. The resulting grids come in all shapes and sizes, because they are determined by how the words can be fitted together as each different alphabet puzzle is built up. For many years we believed that the same grid could not possibly occur twice. That was until 1987, when we were able to produce the puzzle below in which we present you with two identical grids and a number of letters in identical positions in each. However, there the similarity ends. The puzzle is to insert in each grid the remaining letters of the alphabet so that each grid uses entirely different words and only the letters inserted have the same position in both grids. We believe that this is the first and only time that such a double-cross alphabet has been achieved.

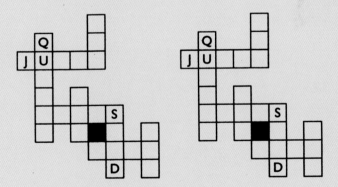

Triple Acrostic

An acrostic is a composition in which the initial letters of the lines taken in order spell out a word or short sentence. Some are written as puzzles, while others make no attempt to conceal the answer. Sometimes the word is based on the last letter of a line (a telestitch), a combination of first and last letters (a double acrostic) or a more complex sequence.

The following is a rarely seen "triple acrostic" in which the solution is based on the initial, middle and final letters of the answer words. The first couplet gives a clue to the answer as a whole and the five numbered couplets provide the five answer words. This acrostic is believed to date from around the middle of this century, but, alas, the author is unknown.

> Left, middle and right
> Give us a choice of light

1. The kind of glance which he who's lost his heart,
   Bestows on her who wears the latter part.

2. Here is one
   With a gun.

3. This is bound,
   To go round.

4. Simplify taste,
   And eliminate waste.

5. My meaning is plain,
   By my saying it again.

Doublets

"Head-Heal-Teal-Tell-Tall-Tail"

The above example was given by Lewis Carroll, the inventor of doublets, when he wrote to the magazine *Vanity Fair* in March 1879 to describe the object of his new puzzle. Carroll had originally called the puzzle Word Links, the object being to find the shortest ladder between a given pair of words by changing one letter at a time. Carroll called the given words "a doublet," the interposed words 'links' and the entire series "a chain" Over the years his puzzle has remained popular and has also been called Laddergrams, Stepwords, Transitions, Transformation, Changelings, Passes, Word Chains, Word Ping-pong and Word Golf. In the following, the first 11 of which were compiled by Carroll, the number of links specified does not include the two doublets—for example, the head-to-tail puzzle above has four links. Recently computers have generated shorter solutions to many of Carroll's puzzles, but we are looking for Carroll's original solutions.

1. Nose to Chin in 5 links

2. Comb to Hair in 6 links

3. Four to Five in 6 links

4. Lion to Lamb in 2 links

5. Pity to Good in 6 links

6. Many to Fail in 7 links

7. Black to White in 5 links

8. Flour to Bread in 5 links

continued

9. River to Shore in 10 links

10. Kettle to Holder in 9 links

11. Grass to Green in 7 links

Finally, in his 1925 *300 Best Word Puzzles*, H. E. Dudeney presents a number of word ladders of his own, of which the following is an example:

12. Kaiser to Porker in 10 links

Twee and Tug

This puzzle was compiled by one of the authors in 1986. It is by no means one of the most difficult of the puzzles we have compiled—in fact, it may be argued that it is one of the easiest. It is a simple substitution cryptogram in which each letter of the alphabet has been substituted for another. We have, however, included it in this collection because of the way in which the substitution has worked to produce an amusing tongue-twisting verse, which bears an uncanny resemblance to how the characters involved would have spoken it. Can you decode the verse?

"FLOP LOPY PLOP?" YOWS TWEE.
"PLU KEOP LOP," YOWS TUG.
"IL, PLOP LOP," YOWS TWEE.
"PLOPY PLOP PLUG."

Nursery Rhyme Crossword 1

The following puzzle was compiled by one of the authors in 1985.

Solve the clues that are hidden in the narrative and place the answers in the correct position in the grid.

"Pussy cat, pussy cat, from the Middle East, with long silky hair and a thick tail, where have you been?"

"I've been to the very middle part of London to see the Queen and Her royal sons, who accuse by legal processes, sets of coordinated doctrines."

"Pussy cat, pussy cat, what did you do there?"

"I frightened some animals with strong incisors with a bend inwards, one of which is snugly embedded under a chair."

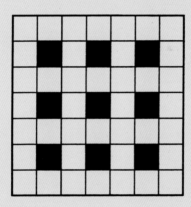

Letter Conundrums

The following conundrums were all compiled between 1850 and 1920. The answer given in each case is a different letter of the alphabet, but in no particular order. Most of these conundrums were researched by the American word expert A. Ross Eckler for his *Word Ways Magazine* of February 1991. Conundrums for the rare letters Q, X and Z are taken from Sam Loyd's 1914 *Cyclopedia of Puzzles*.

Example: What letter is like London?

Answer: E, because it is the capitol of England.

1. What letter is like an island?

2. What letter adds great value to a pear?

3. What letter has the same effect as thunder?

4. What letter is like a cow's tail?

5. What letter is like a schoolmaster?

6. What letter is like a selfish friend?

7. What letter comes once in a minute, twice in a moment and never in a thousand years?

8. What letter is like a scandalmonger?

9. What letter is like a mystery?

10. What letter is like a guide?

11. What letter is like a buck's tail?

12. What letter is the center of joy and the principal mover of sorrow?

13. What letter is like death?

14. What letter widens a road?

15. What letter cannot be seen?

16. What letter is invisible yet never out of sight?

17. What letter changes the sex of a lad?

18. What letter is like noon?

19. What letter is like a pig's tail?

20. What letter is like the sun?

21. What letter is like a wedding ring?

22. What letter is the cleanest in the alphabet?

23. What letter is always the center of mirth?

24. What letter is like the monkey cage?

25. What letter is always discovered in the center of a maze?

26. What letter is like New Year's Day?

Riddles

Both these riddles were composed by the redoubtable Hurbert Phillips. In each case you are looking for a one-word answer. Both riddles are very solvable.

1. My first wears my second; my third might be/What my first would acquire if he went to sea/Put together my one, two, three/And the belle of New York is the girl for me.

2. No hard decode, and, in this case/A solid answer you can claim/It has (I'm told) a different face/For every letter of its name.

Classic Anagrams

Throughout the past one hundred years or so, inventing anagrams has been a popular pastime. In the following all answers bear some relationship to the original. The name of the compiler and date of compilation is given, where known after each. An asterisk indicates a capitalized name in the answer or part of the answer. The answer could be a name, just one word or a phrase.

1. *Genuine class (Dick Cavatt)
2. To scan a visible star or moon (V. E. Beckley)
3. I cry that I sin (Henry B. Wheatley, 1862)
4. No city dust here (Susan Eagleton, 1948)
5. Does ease thirst (David Schulman, 1936)
6. A rope ends it (H. H. Bailey, 1920)
7. Darn it! It is gone (William B. Kirk, 1911)
8. Docile, as a man tamed it (Mrs. Bardwell, 1913)
9. Edge tools (E. J. McIlvane, 1907)
10. Helps theology ("Awl Wrong", 1941)
11. A thousand islets shine (Norman E. Nelson, 1925)
12. Bold hearts fought in Kent ("Amaranth", 1901)
13. English in flight, made port ("Viking", 1931)
14. Quit! I rob health (McCullough B. Wilson, 1915)
15. *Radium came (S. James Nesi, 1936)
16. Gave us a damned clever satire (George W. Heywood, 1898)
17. Stop an ingress (D. C. Ver, 1898)
18. Reaps the blame for losing (Dr. Arthur F. Klaycamp, 1908)
19. *Any labor I do wants time (H. E. Dudeney)
20. *Hasten on to fair Charlotte (Su San, 1934)

Antigrams

An antigram is a rearrangement of letters in a word or phrase into another word or phrase that is opposite in meaning. In the following you are looking for, in each case, an appropriate antigram. Where known, the name of the compiler and date of compilation are given in brackets. An asterisk indicates a capitalized name.

1. A more mild act — (H. Grady Peerey, 1952)
2. Over fifty
3. Evil's agents — (Everett Ewing, 1927)
4. Arch saints — (Dr. W. L. Sacrey, 1931)
5. Nice to imports — ("Hercules", 1928)
6. On the sly
7. Care is noted — (D. C. Ver, 1916)
8. Mad policy — ("Jernand", 1916)
9. *Gains power
10. I won't hear this — (James Lloyd Hood, 1964)

The Urban Riddle

Can you solve the following riddle, which was devised by John Edward Field in 1871?

Come near, o men of wisdom, and search you through
my ditty:
Four buried in this rubbish cities fair are lying low,
Search 'till on every line you see stand up a risen city.
'Till walls and arches, terraces and turrets, upward grow.

MIGHTY BRAINBENDERS

All puzzles are mighty brainbenders, especially if you cannot solve them. However, the ones we have chosen for this section are all, in our opinion, very difficult.

We think that one of the most difficult of all puzzles to comprehend is the Game of Logic, which was first published by Lewis Carroll in 1886. Originally intended for a childhood audience, it has since been conceded that most of these puzzles are "university graduate standard." The object is to deduce one single conclusion from all the statements given. The secret is to take from the series given any two statements with a common term and to draw a conclusion from them. The result is then combined with another premise from the series with a common term and another conclusion reached. You continue thus until only two statements remain, which then yield the ultimate conclusion.

Let us take, for example, one of Carroll's simpler examples:

1. No one takes in *The Times* unless he is well-educated.

2. No hedgehogs can read.

3. Those who cannot read are not well-educated.

Suppose we examine premises 1 and 3. We might conclude that no one who cannot read takes in *The Times*. Then, if you combine this conclusion with premise 2, you might conclude that "No hedgehogs take in *The Times*," and this is exactly the solution that Carroll intended.

Now try the following, which was also compiled by Lewis Carroll. The answer is given as Mighty Brainbenders Introduction.

1. The only animals in this house are cats.

2. Every animal is suitable for a pet, that loves to gaze at the moon.

3. When I detest an animal, I avoid it.

4. No animals are carnivorous, unless they prowl at night.

5. No cat fails to kill mice.

6. No animals ever take to me, except that are in this house.

7. Kangaroos are not suitable for pets.

8. None but carnivora kill mice.

9. I detest animals that do not take to me.
10. Animals that prowl at night, always love to gaze at the moon.

Envelopes

The following puzzle was originated by Nicholas Bernoulli (1695-1726), who was one of the famous family of Swiss mathematicians from Basle.

A correspondent writes seven letters and addresses seven envelopes, one for each letter. In how many ways can all of the letters be placed in wrong envelopes?

The Ultimate Counterfeit Coin Puzzle

We have seen several good counterfeit coin puzzles but this is, we believe, the best and most complex of them all. It is a very old puzzle and, unfortunately, the author is unknown.

In a pile of 12 coins there is a single counterfeit coin, which can be detected only by its weight. Using a balance scale, how can you identify the counterfeit coin in only three operations and determine whether it is heavy or light?

The Knight's Dance

This ancient puzzle from Europe was posed by Guarini Di Forli and dates from 1512.

Make the two white knights change places with the two black knights in the least number of moves.

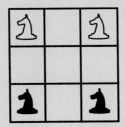

The Square of Fibonacci

Leonardo of Pisa (c.1175-1250), otherwise known as Fibonacci, is famous for the series of numbers (0, 1, 1, 2, 3, 5, 8, 13, 21, 34, etc.) that bears his name. The puzzle that created this series—"How many pairs of rabbits will be produced in a year, beginning with a single pair, if in every month each pair bears a new pair which becomes productive from the second month on?'—is propounded in his book on mathematics, *Liber Abaci* (Book of the Abacus). That work also contains the following puzzle, said to be put to Fibonacci in 1225 by the Emperor Frederick II, who had come to Pisa to test Fibonacci's reputation.

Find a square that remains a square when it is decreased by 5 or increased by 5.

Dodgson's Podgson's Pillow Problem No. 31

Between 1874 and 1891 Lewis Carroll compiled what are known as his pillow problems, later to be published in May 1893 as Part II of Curiosa Mathematica. The one we present here, the thirty-first of such problems, was compiled on March 14, 1889. Carroll would compile the problems while lying awake at night, then in the morning he would write down the answer, followed by the question and then the detailed solution. just one warning about the puzzle that follows: don't expect the answer you are looking for to have nice round figures—Carroll worked out his answer to minute fractions of a second.

On 1 July at 8 a.m. by my watch; it was 4 minutes past 8 a.m. by my clock. I went to Greenwich and, when my watch said noon, the true GMT was 5 minutes past noon. That evening, when my watch said 6 o'clock, the clock said one minute to 6 p.m.

On 30 July, at 9 a.m. by my watch, it was 3 minutes to 9 by my clock. At Greenwich, when my watch said 10 minutes past noon, the true GMT was 5 minutes past 12. That evening, when my watch said 7 p.m., the clock said 2 minutes to 7 p.m.

My watch is only wound up for each journey and goes uniformly during any one day; the dock is always going, and goes uniformly. How am I to know when it is true noon on 31 July?

"Swiftly I Come"

Jonathan Swift (1667-1745) was an Anglo-Irish clergyman, poet and satirist whose masterpiece was *Gulliver's Travels* (1726). He was author of the following riddle.

By something form'd, I nothing am,
Yet Wry thing that you can name;
In no place have I ever been,
Yet everywhere I may be seen;
In all things false, yet always true,
I'm still the same—but never new,
Lifeless, Life's perfect form I wear,
Can show a Nose, Eye, Tongue, or Ear;
Yet neither Smell, See, taste, or Hear.
All Shapes and Features I can boast,
No Flesh, no Bones, no Blood - no Ghost:
All colours, without Paint, put on,
And change like the Cameleon,
Swiftly I come and enter there.
Where not a chink lets in the Air:
Like thought I'm in a Moment gone,
Nor can I ever be alone:
All things on Earth I imitate,
Faster than Nature can create;
Sometimes imperial Robes I wear,
Anon in Beggar's Rags appear:
A Giant now, and strait an Elf.
I'm Wry one, but ne'er myself;
Ne'er said I mourn, ne'er glad rejoice,
I move my Lips, but want a Voice;
I ne'er was born, nor e'er can die,
Then prythee tell me what am I?

Cricket

The following puzzle was devised by one of the authors, who obtained the idea for it from an earlier, much more complicated puzzle, involving palindromic numbers.

The local team used 16 players during the season. The total score for each of the 16 players for the season was a different palindromic prime. None of the players scored a total number that was a five-digit prime, and all of them except one scored three 4s at least, except one player who scored two 4s and his total was of only two digits. When the 16 players' totals are added and then divided by 16 to reach an average, the average is a three-figure number, which consists of the same digit repeated three times.

What was the average?

Note: A palindromic number is one that reads the same backwards or forwards. A prime number is one which is greater than 1, and which has no factors other than 1 and itself. An example of a palindromic prime number is 181.

Hyakugo-Gen

This puzzle appears in the old Chinese book *Sonshi Sankyo* (Mathematical Bible of Military Science) and in several Japanese books on mathematics written between the sixteenth and nineteenth centuries.

You offer to guess someone's age and take them through the following stages:

1. Ask them to divide their age by 3 and tell you the remainder. Say, for example, it is 2.

2. Ask them to divide their age by 5 and tell you the remainder. Say, for example, it is 1.

3. Ask them to divide their age by 7 and tell you the remainder. Say, for example, it is 6.

From this information you correctly calculate that their age is 41. How is this done?

Roll-a-Penny

This puzzle was devised by one of the authors who remembered seeing the "roll-a-penny" game at fairgrounds many years ago.

Repeating pattern

4	4	4	4
4	6	8	4
4	8	10	4
4	4	4	4

2in

1in

We all remember the old fairground game, which is still to be found, where the object is to roll a coin down a chute to land in a square without touching the lines to win the prize in the square in which it has landed.

How does one calculate the chances of winning?

Above is an example of a typical linoleum-topped barker's table on which the game is played. What are the odds against the punter winning?

The coin is 1 inch in diameter and the squares are 2 x 2 inches.

King

The following puzzle was originated by the English scholar Alcuin, who spent his life at the court of Charlemagne.

A king ordered his servant to collect an army from 30 manors in such a way that from each manor he would take the same number of men as he had collected up to then. The servant went to the first manor alone; to the second he went with one other.

How many men were collected in all?

Bezzel's Eight Queens Problem

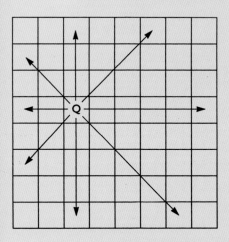

It was in 1848 that a certain Max Bezzel proposed what is now known as the problem of the eight queens when he asked: "What is the largest number of queens that can be placed on an 8 x 8 chess board in such a way that no queen is attacked by another?" As anyone with a basic knowledge of chess will immediately deduce, this means that no two queens must be in the same row, column or diagonal because, of course, the queen, being the most powerful piece in the game of chess, can move any distance in any direction in a straight line as shown in the diagram.

Although it was soon determined how many pieces were necessary, it was not until 1850 that the total number of possible solutions (not counting rotations and reflections of the same solution) was published, and not until 1874 that the proof was published by the English mathematician J. W. L. Glaisher.

Can you determine the following?

1. The largest number of queens that can be placed.

2. The number of possible different solutions.

CLASSIC KICKSELF

A stick I found that weighed two pound:
I sewed it up one day
In pieces of eight of equal weight!
How much did each piece weigh?
—*Lewis Carroll*

The term "kickself puzzle" was said to have been coined at a Mensa dinner in Cambridge some years ago when science fiction writer Arthur C. Clarke asked inventor Sir Clive Sinclair: "What was the first human artefact to break the sound barrier?" There was a brief pause before Clive Sinclair gave the correct answer. (Classic Kickself Introduction 1)

However, as can be seen from the rhyme above, kickself type puzzles–those where you kick yourself when you hear the answer–have been around for many years. The question posed above by Lewis Carroll looks to be the simplest mathematical question imaginable, a simple matter of dividing two by eight, but as might be expected it is not quite that simple, as you will see if you turn to (Classic Kickself Introduction 2).

Perhaps the first kickself puzzle was the one in Greek legend which was propounded by the Sphinx: "What walks on four legs in the morning, two legs in the afternoon and three legs in the evening?" Scores of would-be solvers had been put to death by the Sphinx for their failure to solve the riddle until Oedipus came to Thebes and won his throne by correctly answering the riddle. Can you solve the riddle of the Sphinx? (Classic Kickself Introduction 3)

Another prominent Mensa member, the late Isaac Asimov, also once weighed in with a great kickself puzzle, which is one of our favourites: "What word in the English language changes its pronunciation when nationalized?" (Classic Kickself Introduction 4)

But perhaps our favorite kickself puzzle is one of Sam Loyd's most famous, which is illustrated below. It shows a map of the newly discovered cities and waterways on our nearest neighbor planet, Mars. Start at the city marked T, at the south pole, and see if you can spell a complete English sentence by making a tour of all the cities, visiting each city once only, and returning to the starting point. When the puzzle appeared in a magazine originally, more than 50,000 readers reported, "there is no possible way," and yet it is a very simple puzzle. Why was that? (Classic Kickself Introduction 5)

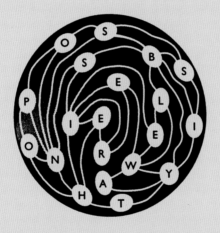

Roll of Cloth

A man has 100 yards of cloth in a single roll, and he wishes to divide it into 100 lengths of 1 yard each. It takes him 3 seconds to cut each length. Working flat-out, non-stop, how long does it take him to cut all 100 pieces?

Tell Me Who

Sometimes a chap'll
   Find, in some trivial happening, inspiration:
The fall of an apple
Led—so 'tis said, a Cambridge don to grapple
   With the mysteries of the Laws of Gravitation.
The Royal Society
Remembers him with piety.

The above was penned by Hubert Phillips for his quiz book *Tell Me Who*, described as a "biographical puzzle game." The answer, of course, is Sir Isaac Newton (1642-1727), who was president of the Royal Society and composer of the following riddle.

Four people sat down at a table to play;
They played all that night, and some part of next day;
This one thing observed, that when all were seated,
Nobody played with them, and nobody betted:
Yet, when they got up, each was winner a guinea;
Who tells me this riddle, I'm sure is no ninny.

Incidentally, we would have loved to have listened to the dialect of Isaac Newton to learn how he managed to get "seated" to rhyme with "betted."

A Simple Equation

Here is another puzzle by Boris Kordemsky, dating from c.1900.

Find a simple method of solving:

$$6751x + 3249y = 26751$$
$$3249x + 6751y = 23249$$

The Elusive Lift

This puzzle was compiled by one of the authors in 1986, and it illustrates how suddenly ideas for puzzles can hit you. The idea came after he had finished work for the day and was relaxing watching the Dave Allen show on television. The comedian started telling a joke about a lift going up and down in a department store and the puzzle idea flashed through his head. He dashed upstairs to his study and committed the following puzzle to paper. He never did hear the end of the joke!

I was on the second floor of a New York department store recently. "Let's take the lift," said my wife. "It won't be long; it's on the third floor and coming down." We waited, but to our annoyance it shot straight past us to floor one, then up to the fourth floor, straight back down to the first again and then back up to the fifth. "This is useless," I said. "Let's walk." "No, hang on for a few more minutes," said my wife. "It will probably continue straight up to the ninth floor and then come straight back down to us." We waited, and sure enough the lift did exactly as my wife had predicted. How did she know?

The Simple Twist

Here is a clever kickself puzzle by H. E. Dudeney.

A ball 13 inches in diameter has a 5-inch hole drilled through the center. How deep is the hole?

5 in

13 in

Where There Is a Will There Is a Way

An Old Lady left $33,333 to be divided equally among two fathers and two sons, and each was to receive $11,111. How was this possible?

Something in Common 1

This puzzle was compiled by one of the authors in 1990.

What have the following in common?

A MINE
A HOLM OAK
A HUT

An Angle on a Cube

AB and BC are two diagonals drawn on the face of a cube. How many degrees is the angle created at ABC?

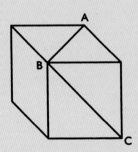

Calendice

Some calendars are very complex, but here is a very simple system by which one can, by using just 12 faces, show all of the 31 days in the month. We show you 5 faces. Your task is to find the numbers that should go on the other 7 faces.

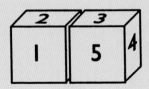

The Crimean Conundrum

The following conundrum was posed by the English Whig statesman Charles James Fox (1749-1806).

I went to the Crimea; I stopped there, and I never went there, and I came back again. What am I?

Carousel

Here is another of Sam Loyd's kickselfs.

While enjoying a giddy ride on the carousel Sammy proposed this problem.

One-third of the number of kids riding ahead of me, added to three-quarters of those riding behind me, gives the correct number of children on this merry-go-round. How many children were riding on the carousel?

PERPLEXITIES

A man is looking at a portrait and he says: "Sisters and brothers have I none, but that man's father is my father's son."

Hubert Phillips once remarked that he had received scores of letters asking him to settle arguments as to whose portrait the man was looking at. Philip's reaction to this was to comment as follows:

"I think it is pathetic that having sufficient interest in abstractions to tackle the problem, my correspondents have not sufficient confidence in their own powers of reasoning to satisfy themselves as to the answer. The only possible explanation is that their capacity to use their wits has fallen into disuse. I have often heard the above 'chestnut' hotly, debated–and by quite intelligent people too. 'It's himself' 'It's his son.' 'It's his grandson.' Yet how few of those participating in such arguments will adopt the obvious line of approach:

"You say it's himself. In that case "that man's father" (i.e., the speaker's father) is also the speaker's father's son. Does that make sense? Or can a man be his own father? And you say, madam, 'It's his grandson.' Let us test your hypothesis. 'That man's father' now becomes the speaker's grandson's father–in other words, the speaker's son. Thus the speaker's son is also the speaker's father's son–i.e., the speaker himself. Does that make sense? And now the answer should be apparent–that the portrait is that of the speaker's son."

Notwithstanding Hubert Phillips' tongue in cheek comments, it is still today a conundrum that catches out many people, and maybe, if you were not confused at the outset, you will be after reading Mr. Phillips' explanation of how to solve the puzzle.

More perplexities follow in this section.

Confusion at the Rectory

The following puzzle was compiled by Hubert Phillips.

The rector's four boys have done their best to make the dog situation at the rectory confusing. Each of the four–their names are Alec, Bob, Charlie and David–owns two dogs, and each has named his dogs after two of his brothers. Each boy has, in consequence, two doggy namesakes.

Of the eight dogs, three are cocker spaniels, three are terriers and two are dachshunds. None of the four boys owns two dogs of the same breed. No two dogs of the same breed have the same name. Neither of Alec's dogs is named David and neither of Charlie's dogs is named Alec. No cocker spaniel is named Alec, and no terrier is named David. Bob does not own a terrier.

Who are the owners, and what are the names, of the dachshunds?

The Village Simpleton

Here is another puzzle from H. E. Dudeney

A facetious individual, who was taking a long walk in the country, came upon a yokel sitting on a stile. As the gentleman was not quite sure of his road, he thought he would make enquiries of the local inhabitant; but at the first glance he jumped too hastily to the conclusion that he had dropped on the village idiot. He, therefore, decided to test the fellow's intelligence first by putting to him the simplest question he could think of, which was: "What day of the week is this, my good man?" The following is the smart answer that he received:

"When the day after tomorrow is yesterday, today will be as far from Sunday as today was from Sunday when the day before yesterday was tomorrow."

Can you say what day of the week it was? It is pretty evident that the countryman was not such a fool as he looked. The gentleman went on the road a puzzled but a wiser man.

The Get off
the Earth Puzzle

Sam Loyd designed the puzzle below in 1896 as an advertisement for Bergen Beach, a newly opened resort in New Jersey, and he regarded it as his greatest puzzle.

The puzzle consists of two concentric pieces of cardboard, fastened together so that the smaller, inner circle pivots backwards and forwards. In the left-hand illustration there are 13 Chinese warriors, but in the right-hand illustration, after the wheel has been turned slightly, there are only 12. The puzzle has generated a great deal of speculation over the years and several explanations have been put forward, including Loyd's 'red herring' that he changed a right leg for a left leg between the fourth and fifth man. What is the explanation?

Tower of Hanoi Patience

There are several legends concerning the origin of this famous puzzle, which was the invention of Edouard Lucas and was sold as a toy in France in 1883. Lucas's version has it that in the great temple of Benares are 64 golden discs of different sizes and mounted on three pillars, two of diamond and one of gold. When he created the universe, the God Brahma placed all 64 discs on one of the diamond pegs in descending order of size, with the largest disc at the bottom. The temple priests had to transfer the discs from one pillar to another. However, a larger disc was never allowed to be placed on top of a smaller disc. As soon as all 64 discs had been transferred to the gold pillar the universe would end. Fortunately for us all, if the priests transferred a disc every second of every day it would take them many millions of years to complete their task. The actual mathematics of the task are that the number of moves required for a given number of discs is 2^{n-1}. Thus 3 discs could be transferred in 7 moves, 5 discs in 31 moves and 16 discs in 65,535 moves, etc.

The card game below is an adaptation of this old puzzle, and nine cards of the same suit are used, from 2 to 10 inclusive. They are laid out in three rows of three as shown. The object is to get the cards to a single column in descending sequence by moving according to the following rules:

1. One card only may be moved at a time.

2. It must be a card from the foot of a column.

3. It can be placed only at the foot of another column and only below a higher card.

When a "vacancy" occurs–i.e., when all the cards in one column have been moved–the bottom card of either of the remaining columns may be used to fill the vacancy.

Virgil's Riddle

Virgil was the sobriquet of Publius Vergilius Maro (70-19 13 B.C.). He was the supreme poet of Imperial Rome and the object of superstitious reverence to later generations. He compiled the following riddle.

Damoetas: Read me this riddle and I shall take you for Apollo's self. "Where in the world is the sky no more than three yards wide?"

Think of a Number

The following puzzle was devised by one of the authors, who adapted it from an earlier, almost impossible puzzle, based on square and cube numbers. This one is much more soluble.

A has thought of a number between 13 and 1300.
B is trying to guess it.
B asks whether the number is below 500.
A says yes.
B asks if the number is a perfect cube.
A says yes.
B asks if the number is a perfect square.
A says yes.
A says that only two of his answers are correct and the number starts with 5, 7 or 9.
B now knows the number.

What is it?

Ages

Jim is 36 years old. He is twice as old as Sid was when he, Jim, was as old as Sid is now. How old was Sid a year ago?

Random Numbers

Ernie' is a random number producer. Pi could also be said to be a random number producer, because the decimal equivalent is known to only 20 million places–nobody knows the hundred-million[th] or million-millionth decimal place. The most unusual feature of an infinite random number is that, for instance, 999999999 must occur somewhere within it, as in fact, must every possible combination of digits that you wish to name. So, if you had a random number sequence, what would be the average difference between two random digits side by side? Strangely enough it is not

$$\frac{0 + 9}{2} = 4^{1}/_{2}$$

Tangrams

The tangram puzzle is probably the most ancient in origin of all dissection puzzles. It is believed to have originated in China 4000 years ago, although the earliest known reference to it is a wood-cut from 1780 by Utamoro, which depicts two courtesans trying to solve *Chi-Chiao* (the Seven Clever Pieces).

The puzzle is made up from seven pieces cut from a square as shown below and the object is to create tangram shapes from the seven pieces.

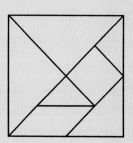

Lewis Carroll was, not surprisingly, fascinated by tangrams and owned a book, *The Fashionable Chinese Puzzle*, which contained 323 tangrams and which, on Carroll's death, passed to H. E. Dudeney. It was Dudeney who, created the following paradox in which he illustrates two Chinamen, apparently identical except for the missing foot on the right-hand figure. However, both figures contain all seven identical tangram pieces. Can you create the two figures with the seven tangram pieces?

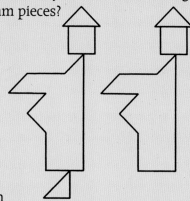

The Two Chinamen

Mad as a Hatter!

The hatter opened his eyes very wide on hearing this; but all he said was, "Why is a raven like a writing desk?" "Come, we shall have some fun now!" thought Alice. "I'm glad they've begun asking riddles–I believe I can guess that," she added aloud.

Lewis Carroll, *Alice's Adventures in Wonderland*

But, Alice never did provide the answer and neither did the hatter. Can you work out an answer to the riddle: "Why is a raven like a writing desk?"

Mad Hatter Tangram (H. E. Dudeney)

Ale Inn Cans Code

Can you decode the following message which was sent, undetected, in 1862 during the American Civil War? Who sent the message?

Burnside, Acquia Creek:
Can Inn Ale me withe 2 oar our Ann pas Ann me flesh ends N.y. Corn Inn out with U cud Inn heaven day nest Wed Roe Moor Tom darkey hat Creek Why Hawk of abbot Inn b chewed I if–Bates.

Intelligence Challengers

Find Another Word

Consider the following list of words:

SEAT
LINE
FOOT
HOUSE

Now choose one of the following words to add to the list:

TABLE
BED
CUPBOARD
WINDOW
FLOOR

The Energetic Dog

A man is walking his dog on the lead towards home at a steady 3 mph. When they are 7 miles from home the man lets his dog off the lead. The dog immediately runs off towards home at 8 mph. When the dog reaches the house it turns around and runs back to the man at the same speed. When it reaches the man it turns back for the house. This is repeated until the man gets home and lets the dog in. How many miles does the dog cover from being let off the lead to being let into the house?

Harem

A sultan tried to increase the number of women available for harems in his country by passing a law forbidding women to have another child once they gave birth to a son; as long as the children were girls they would be permitted to continue childbearing. "Under this new law," the sultan explained, "you will see women having families such as four girls and one boy; ten girls and one boy; perhaps a solitary boy, and so on. This should obviously increase the ratio of women to men."

Is this true?

Wot! No Vowels

Find 14 words of three or more letters contained in the grid. Words run in any direction, backward and forward, horizontal, vertical and diagonal, but only in a straight line.

Y	P	M	Y	L	S
S	R	H	X	Y	P
L	H	T	Z	M	Y
Y	S	Y	L	P	H
L	G	H	L	H	W
Y	H	R	R	Y	M

Odd One Out 2

Which is the odd one out?

AIL
NOT
ROW
INCH
LOVER
THREAD

Figure It Out

There is a single feature that these words have in common.
What is it?

ENUMERATE
UNOCCUPIED
ONEROUS
UNUSUAL
BIRD

Shooting Match

Victor, Madsen and David each fired six shots, and each got 7 points. Victor's first two shots scored 22 points and Madsen's first shot scored only 3 points.

Who hit the bull's-eye?

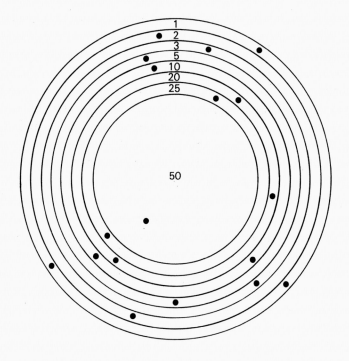

Square

Divide the square into four identical sections. Each section must contain the same nine letters, which can be arranged into a nine-letter word.

O	P	C	N	C	P
C	Y	H	O	Y	O
C	P	A	C	O	N
H	N	O	C	A	H
A	Y	P	H	Y	O
O	C	A	N	O	C

ANAGRAMS

To the purist a true anagram is a word or phrase the letters of which can be rearranged into another word or phrase which bears some relationship to the original. Our first puzzle in the section, Appropriate Anagrams, is a good illustration of this type of word play.

If you are a devotee of anagrams, you are in good company: Queen Victoria, for instance, was very fond of them. Here is one teaser which was said to have stumped her. Rearrange the letters of "ABONETY" into a seven-letter word (this may not be as easy as it at first appears). See how quickly you are able to come up with the correct solution. (See Anagrams Introduction of Intelligence Challengers)

Appropriate Anagrams

All the solutions to the following have some relationship with the original. Numbers in parentheses refer to number of letters in each word of the solution.

1. They see (3, 4)

2. Truss neatly to be safe (6, 4, 4, 5)

3. Bear hit den (10)

4. I batch words (11)

5. Sear sad earth (6, 6)

6. Many a sad heart can whisper my prayer
(1, 5, 9, 3, 1, 5, 3, 4)

7. HMS Pinafore (4, 3, 4)

8. I love Ms. Nude (5, 2, 4)

Enigmasig 1

Complete the words in each column, all of which end in E. The scrambled letters in the section to the right of each column are an anagram of a word which will give you a clue to the word you are trying to find to put in the column.

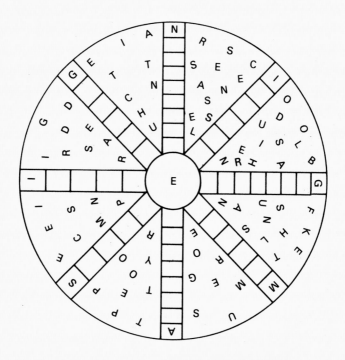

Enigmasig 2

Complete the words in each column, all of which end in E. The scrambled letters in the section to the right of each column are an anagram of a word which will give you a clue to the word you are trying to find to put in the column.

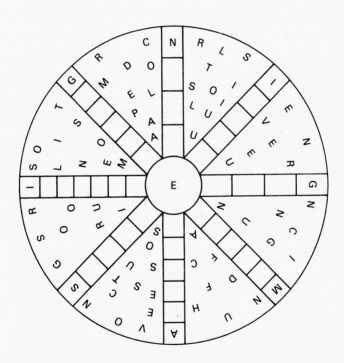

Anagram Themes

In each set below arrange the 14 words in pairs so that each pair is an anagram of another word or name. The seven words produced will have a linking theme. For example, if the words DIAL and THAN were in the list they could be paired to form an anagram of THAILAND, the theme being countries.

(a) BE	(b) AGE
COIN	FEAR
HE	GILD
HOLD	HAND
LAW	MAID
NEAT	MAT
PAD	MORE
PIN	NO
RATE	RAN
RAVE	RIG
ROLE	RUN
RUM	SHOWING
TASK	SON
UPPER	TAN

No Neighbors

In each of the following, unscramble the letters to find a word. There are no two adjoining letters in the same shape.

(a) 13-letter word

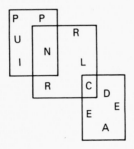

(b) 11 -letter word

(c) 12-letter word

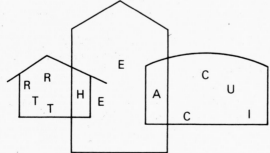

Anagrammed Synonyms

In each of the following, study the three words given. Your task is to pair two of them to form an anagram of a word which is a synonym of the word remaining.

For example: DEED - EMPTY - REST. The words DEED and REST are an anagram of DESERTED, which is a synonym of the remaining word, EMPTY.

1. OPEN - APRON - FAIR

2. WHEEL - SEER - OUT

3. CALL - MAIL - CROP

4. MAR - SEND - STINT

5. TAME - PEER - SOAK

6. MET - SOBER - REPEAT

7. LEG - MEEK - NET

8. CASE - LATE - DEED

9. GAIN - BEAD - WIT

10. SAND - DART - PAR

11. CUR - HEAD - MAIN

12. HOP - CUP - TRY

13. SMELL - LONE - CREED

14. SAD - PEACE - LARK

Enigmagram

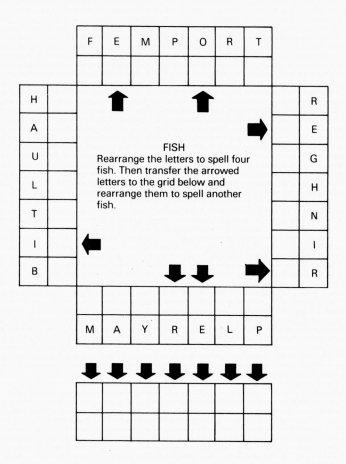

F	E	M	P	O	R	T

FISH

Rearrange the letters to spell four fish. Then transfer the arrowed letters to the grid below and rearrange them to spell another fish.

H		R
A		E
U		G
L		H
T		N
I		I
B		R

M	A	Y	R	E	L	P

NUMBERS

Numbers can be challenging, fascinating, confusing and frustrating, but once you have developed an interest in them, a whole new world is opened up as you discover their many characteristics and patterns. Numbers can be divided into many different categories: a few of these, which we would like to expound on, are amicable, abundant, deficient, perfect and delectable numbers.

Amicable numbers are pairs which are mutually equal to the sum of all their aliquot parts: for example, 220 and 284. The aliquot parts of 220 are 1, 2, 4, 5, 10, 11, 20, 22, and 110, the sum of which is 284, while the aliquot parts of 284 are 1, 2, 4, 75 and 142, the sum of which is 220. There are seven known pairs of amicable numbers, the largest of which are 9,437,056 and 7,363,584.

Abundant, deficient and perfect numbers can be linked together, as every number is one of these. An abundant number is one such that the sum of all its divisors (except itself) is greater than the number itself: for example, 12, because its divisors, 1, 2, 3,4 and 6, total 16. The opposite of this is a deficient number, where the divisors total less than the number itself: for example, 10, whose divisors, 1, 2 and 5, total 8. If a number is not abundant or deficient, then it must be perfect, which means that it is equal to the sum of its aliquot parts: for example, 6, where its divisors, 1, 2, and 3, also total 6. Perfect numbers were first named in Ancient Greece by the Pythagoreans around 500 B.C. and to date only 30 have been discovered. The first four perfect numbers were discovered before A.D.100 and these are 6, 28, 496 and 8, 128. However, the next was not found until the fifteenth century; it is 33,550,336. With the help of computer technology, the process of discovering new perfect numbers has been speeded up and the latest to be found has no fewer than 240 digits. One fact that has emerged is that all the perfect numbers now known are even numbers. However, no one from the time of Euclid to the present day has been able to prove that it is mathematically impossible for a perfect odd number to exist.

So, having dealt with amicable, abundant, deficient and perfect numbers, what, may you ask, is a delectable number? The answer is that a nine-digit number is delectable if (a) it contains the digits 1 to 9 exactly once each (no zero) and (b) the numbers created by taking the first n digits (n runs from 1 to 9) are each divisible by n, so the first digit is divisible by 1 (it always will be), the first two digits form a number divisible by 2, the first three digits form a number divisible by 3, and so on. It is known that there is one, and only one, number which meets the above conditions and can be called a delectable number. Can you find out what it is? (See Numbers Introduction of Intelligence Challengers)

Connections 1

Insert the numbers 0 to 10 in the circles, so that for any particular circle the sum of the numbers in the circles connected directly to it equals the value corresponding to the number in that circle as given in the list below.

For example:

$1 = 14 \ (4 + 7 + 3)$

$4 = 8 \ (7 + 1)$

$7 = 5 \ (4 + 1)$

$3 = 1$

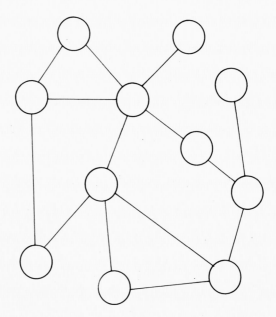

$0 = 13$

$1 = 8$

$2 = 11$

$3 = 15$

$4 = 8$

$5 = 25$

$6 = 7$

$7 = 20$

$8 = 20$

$9 = 12$

$10 = 0$

Average Speed

A car travels at a speed of 50 mph over a certain distance and then returns over the same distance at a speed of 30 mph. What is the average speed for the total journey?

Train

A train travelling at a speed of 0 mph enters a tunnel which is $1^1/_2$ miles long. The length of the train is $^1/_4$ mile. How long does it take for all of the train to pass through the tunnel, from the moment the front enters to the moment the rear emerges?

Fractions

(a) Arrange the digits 1 to 9 once each only to form a single fraction that equals one eighth.

(b) Arrange the digits 1 to 9 once each only to form a single fraction that equals one seventh.

(c) Arrange the digits 1 to 9 once each only to form a single fraction that equals one sixth.

(d) Arrange the digits 1 to 9 once each only to form a single fraction that equals one half.

Horse Racing

4.00 Everingham Maiden Stakes

1. Anfield's Star	5-2
2. Fresh from Victory	7-2
3. James Star	9-2
4. King of Sailors	5-1
5. Lapiaffe	10-1
6. Mariner's Law	16-1
7. Turture	20-1
8. Dayadari	?

What odds should the bookmaker give against Dayadari to give himself a 10 per cent margin on the race, assuming he balanced his books?

Lathe

A lathe turner reduced the time taken to process a metal part from 35 minutes to $2^1/_2$ minutes. He increased his cutting speed by 1690 inches per minute. To how much?

Coin

Three men, A, B and C, toss a coin in succession. The winner will be the first to throw a head. What are their respective chances?

Dice

How many times on average must an ordinary six-sided die be tossed before every number from 1 to 6 comes up at least once?

Numbers 1

What is the missing number in this list?

1
64
125
216
729
13, 824
15, 625
?
13, 2651

Square Numbers 1

Each horizontal and vertical line contains the digits of a four-figure square number. The digits are always in the right order, but not necessarily adjacent. Each digit is used once only, and they are all used. Find the 16 four-figure square numbers.

4	1	6	7	4	8	9	9
2	1	5	2	4	2	5	3
9	1	4	9	7	5	6	1
2	5	8	2	6	0	9	2
1	3	6	9	6	9	6	9
6	5	3	2	2	2	0	9
4	6	2	2	4	5	4	4
3	1	1	1	3	9	6	9

Cinderella

Cinderella has 89 buttons. There are six lots—5-6-12-14-23-29—each a different shade, but only two colors–red and blue. The ugly sisters took away one lot, leaving twice as many reds as blues. Which lot was taken?

Series 1

What is the missing number in this series?

1, 81, 2025, 3025, 9801, 88209, ?, 998001, 4941729

Spot on the Table

A boy, recently home from school, wished to give his father an exhibition of his precocity. He pushed a large circular table into the corner of the room, so that it touched both walls, and he then pointed to a spot of ink on the extreme edge.

"Here is a little puzzle for you, Pater," said the youth. "That spot is exactly 8 inches from one wall and 9 inches from the other. Can you tell me the diameter of the table without measuring it?"

The boy was overheard to tell a friend, "It fairly beat the guv'nor", but his father is known to have remarked to a City acquaintance that he solved the thing in his head in a minute. I often wonder which spoke the truth.

Handshakes

If 20 people, on parting, all shake hands with each other once, how many handshakes will there be altogether?

Odd Number

Select two positive integers at random, A + D, such that A < D. Select two more positive integers at random, B + C, such that A < B < C <D.

For example: 68 - 187 - 1667 - 2095

Are the chances that B + C = an odd number:

50 per cent?
less than 50 per cent?
more than 50 per cent?

Look Alike

Find the smallest possible number which when multiplied by 29 looks the same as it did before, but with the addition of the same digit on each end.

For example: ABC X 29 = YABCY

WORD PLAY

It is often said that to have a mastery of words is to have in one's possession the ability to produce order out of chaos and that command of vocabulary is a true measure of intelligence. As such, vocabulary tests are widely used in intelligence testing.

Here are a few examples of word play for you to try before tackling the rest of our word puzzles in this section. (See Word Play Introduction of Intelligence Challengers)

Find in the English language:

1. A word which, without a change in pronunciation, has two directly contrary meanings;

2. A seven-letter word which contains each of the five vowels once;

3. An 11-letter word whose odd letters spell out a word and whose even letters spell out a word;

4. A nine-letter word which is an anagram of a state of the USA;

5. The only word to have the letters UFA embedded in it;

6. A word having five consecutive vowels embedded in it;

7. Two words which are synonyms when used as verbs but antonyms when used as adjectives, adverbs or nouns;

8. The longest word which can be typed on the top row of a typewriter.

Pyramid

Using the following letters only, fill in the pyramid so that each horizontal line forms a word. Use each letter as many times as necessary. Each word formed must consist of the same letters as the word above it, in any order, plus one additional letter.

A, E, L, N, R, S, T

nine-letter word base

Something in Common 2

What do the following words have in common?

HONOR
CHECK
THEATER
LICENSE
CENTER

Alphabet

Use the 26 letters of the alphabet once each to complete these words.

ABCDEFGHIJKLMNOPQRSTUVWXYZ

1. D---

2. -O-E

3. -AL-R-

4. HA-E

5. -U--A-

6. -A-

7. -UA--

8. -O-

9. -A--A

10. -O--

Square Words

Spiral clockwise around the perimeter and finish at the center square to spell out the nine-letter words. Each word commences at one of the four corner squares.

(a)

A		C
	E	A
I	T	

(b)

	U	
S	E	T
O		A

(c)

	G	
I	D	I
K	E	

(d)

B		S
E	R	
	N	A

(e)

R		U
U	E	O
	S	

Labyrinth

In each of the following, spell out the 15-letter word by going through the labyrinth one room at a time. Go into each room once only. You may go into the corridor as many times as you wish.

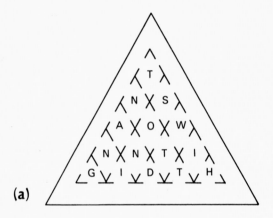

(a)

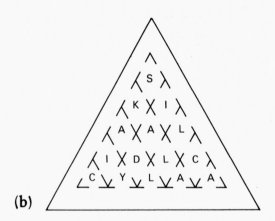

(b)

Word Construction 1

Use all the 30 small words scattered below once each only to construct 10 words (three small words per word).

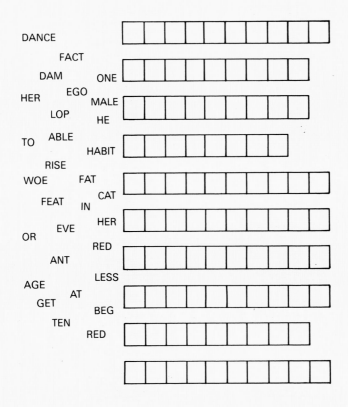

DANCE

FACT

DAM   ONE

EGO

HER   MALE

LOP   HE

TO   ABLE

HABIT

RISE

WOE   FAT

FEAT   CAT

IN

EVE   HER

OR

RED

ANT

LESS

AGE

AT

GET

BEG

TEN

RED

Track Words

Fill in the spaces to find the words. All letters are in the correct order and the overlapping letter appears twice. The word might appear reading clockwise or counterclockwise.

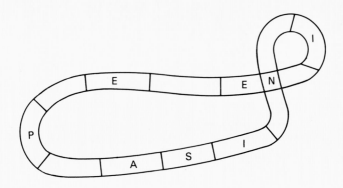

(a) 15-letter word

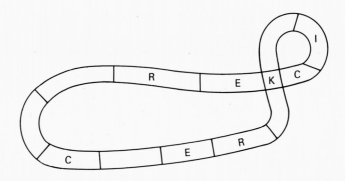

(b) 14-letter word

Cryptic Elimination 1

Each clue is solved by joining together two words from the 25 listed. You will use 24 words. Find the odd word left over.

A. Does this recluse use a gin in his grounds?
B. Thigh-slapping transvestite.
C. In charge of the road works.
D. 72 makeshift people who are biased.
E. Does this marauder of the deep like the sun?
F. Charge for the cutlery and get the bird.
G. Difficult to get Jackson out unless the bowler is Hadrian.
H. Hire the knight, the price looks good.
I. This bird will do well in the marathon.
J. Sounds like an irritable monster.
K. Russian sea-faring lepidopterist.
L. Put the government away for the duration.

1. Admiral
2. Basking
3. Bill
4. Boy
5. Cabinet
6. Dragon
7. Drill
8. Filing
9. Free
10. Jury
11. Lance
12. Monk
13. Principal
14. Red
15. Rigged
16. Road
17. Runner
18. Sergeant
19. Shark
20. Snap
21. Spoon
22. Squash
23. Stone
24. Trappist
25. Wall

Cryptic Elimination 2

Each clue is solved by joining together two words from the 25 listed. You will use 24 words. Find the odd word left over.

A. A bird for the winter season.
B. A simple movement in dancing.
C. Furry creature with a ringer? No, it's a plant.
D. You would expect to see the bird flying.
E. This mammal could mean murder.
F. Starting point for a race on board ship.
G. Hat worn when hunting animals.
H. Stuck up! Should try eating sweets properly.
I. Opposite of open-handed.
J. It may bounce in the post office.
K. Rapid writing system for 5-foot worker.
L. Female advertising executive in orbit.

1. Bell	**14.** Side
2. Deer	**15.** Silver
3. Fisted	**16.** Snow
4. Goose	**17.** Space
5. Hand	**18.** Stalker
6. Hare	**19.** Stamp
7. Jay	**20.** Step
8. Killer	**21.** Tight
9. Line	**22.** Toffee
10. Nosed	**23.** Walking
11. Plimsoll	**24.** Whale
12. Rubber	**25.** Woman
13. Short	

Fours

Place a four-letter word in the center so that when added on to the end of the first four-letter word it will produce an eight-letter word, and when placed in front of the second four-letter word it will produce another eight-letter word.

1. WORM ---- AWAY
2. FOLK ---- BIRD
3. BACK ---- ROOM
4. CLUB ---- BALL
5. TURN ---- LAND
6. FORE ---- PLAY
7. DOWN ---- SIDE
8. WOOD ---- MILL
9. GOLD ---- HOUR
10. TYPE ---- LIFT

Pair Words

Here are two lists of words. Each word in List A has two possible pair words in List B. Each word in List B has two possible pair words in List A. There are two possible solutions. Pair a word from each list until you have eight pairs.

List A		List B	
NUPTIALS	MAIDEN	RING	WEDDING
SOLE	TOREADOR	HORSE	MATADOR
BULL	SEA	SEVILLE	LEMON
DIAMOND	ORANGE	SWORDFISH	NUBILE

Word Circle

In the example a circle of three six-letter words–oncost, stripe and person–each overlap by two letters. Each word is divided into two-letter groups and these two-letter groups from the circle are arranged in alphabetical order, that is, GO, ON, PE, RI, RS, ST.

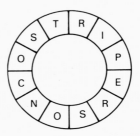

Now try to unscramble the following to find a circle of eight six-letter words, each word overlapping its neighbor by two letters.

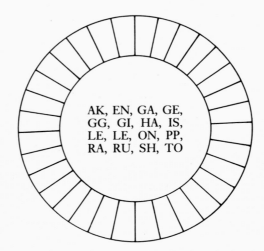

AK, EN, GA, GE, GG, GI, HA, IS, LE, LE, ON, PP, RA, RU, SH, TO

Hexwords

Fit the words into the six spaces around each black center, either clockwise or counterclockwise, so that all the words link up.

TYPING
BOVINE
PANDER
GROVES
GINGER
NINETY
SEVENS
PASSES
SPACES
SEDANS
COBALT
LANDED

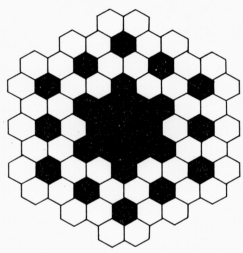

Pathway

Find seven words each commencing with the central letter K. Words are in adjacent squares in any direction and each letter is used once only.

O	O	S	L	T	B	U
A	R	S	E	T	B	T
G	N	A	E	I	N	Z
E	R	I	**K**	I	K	A
H	N	O	A	I	O	J
S	G	L	R	E	B	U
I	F	N	I	Z	T	I

DIAGRAMS

The puzzles here are not tests of numeracy or literacy but concern diagrammatic representation. Widely used in intelligence testing, diagrammatic tests are considered to be culture-fair and test raw intelligence without the influence of prior knowledge. They will probe your understanding of space relationships, pattern and design. At first some of these puzzles may appear daunting, but our advice is to stick with them, because after careful study the solution may suddenly appear to you. As with all the puzzles in this book, please do not rush to look up the answer if you cannot see a solution immediately. Remember that a puzzle which baffles you initially may suddenly seem soluble if you take a fresh look some time later. Puzzles, to a great extent, are like problems in life: they often need to be worked at and thought about before the reward of a successful solution is obtained.

Logic 1

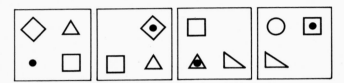

Which of the following continues the above sequence?

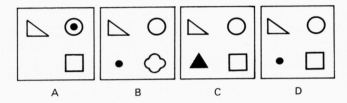

A   B   C   D

Odd One Out 2

Which of the following is the odd one out?

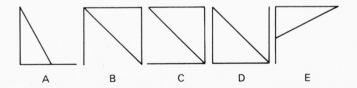

A   B   C   D   E

Advanced Matrix

Look along each line horizontally and then down each line vertically to find what, logically, should be in the missing square.

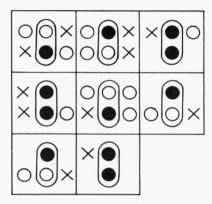

Choose from:

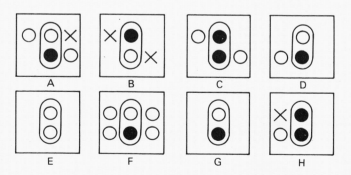

Conditions

Study the three rectangles below. Which one of the options given has the most in common with them?

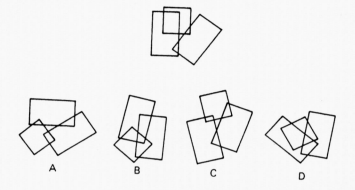

A   B   C   D

Target

Which of the following continues the above sequence?

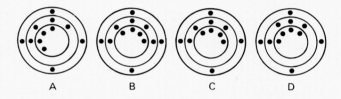

A   B   C   D

Squares

In both of the following, divide the squares into four parts of equal size and shape in such a way that each shape includes one of each of the four symbols.

(a)

(b)

QUOTATIONS

For us one of the joys in compiling puzzles is to root out good quotations, and you will find several sprinkled throughout this book. We find that quotations can be thought-provoking, appropriate and amusing and we hope that you will share our enjoyment of them.

Knight's Move

Start at the letter T in the bottom right-hand corner and by knight's moves spell out a quotation by Blaise Pascal.

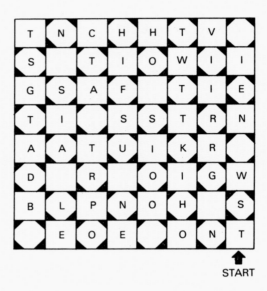

START

In chess the knight is the only piece allowed to jump over other pieces. It can move one square horizontally and two vertically or two horizontally and one vertically (as in the diagram to the right). Usually represented by a horse's head, it is occasionally referred to as the horse (as in the Arabic version).

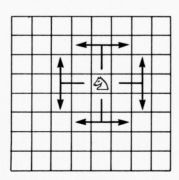

Quotation Pyramid

"Let's get out of these wet clothes and into a dry martini."
Using all 45 letters of the above quotation by Robert
Benchley, complete the pyramid. Across clues are given, but
in no particular order.

CLUES:

Travel

Avoided deliberately

Neuter pronoun of
the third person

Military pageant

In good health

Fireproof cooking dish

Pronoun of the first person
singular

Short sacred vocal composition

Indifferent dullness

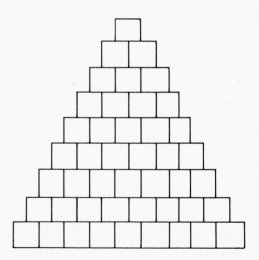

Quotation

The grid contains a quotation by Francis Bacon. The letters in the columns go into the squares above. You have to select which squares.

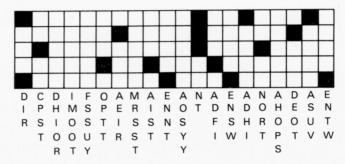

```
D   C   D   I   F   O   A   M   A   E   A   N   A   E   A   N   A   D   A   E
I   P   H   M   S   P   E   R   I   N   O   T   D   N   D   O   H   E   S   N
R   S   I   O   S   T   I   S   N   O   T       F   S   H   R   O   O   U   T
T   O   O   U   T   R   S   S   T   S   Y       I   W   I   T   P   T   V   W
    R   T   Y       T       T       T   Y           W       P   S
                                                            S
```

Acrostic

Solve the clues and fill in the answers in the grid overleaf (the clues are in order). Then transfer the letters from the answers to their corresponding numbers in the square grid below it to reveal a quotation. The name of the author can be found by reading down the first vertical column of answers.

CLUES:

Cogitate

Take a piece at draughts

Shaft of wood with broad blade

Nutritious seed

Power

Avoid

Stopped ball with body

One of the Three Musketeers

Deep narrow gorge

One or other of two

Move tail vigorously

MAGIC SQUARES

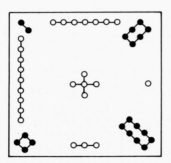

1. The Loh River 15

52	61	4	13	20	29	36	45
14	3	62	51	46	35	30	19
53	60	5	12	21	28	37	44
11	6	59	54	43	38	27	22
55	58	7	10	23	26	39	42
9	8	57	56	41	40	25	24
50	63	2	15	18	31	34	47
16	1	64	49	48	33	32	17

2. The Franklin 260

Magic number squares have intrigued mathematicians and puzzle fanatics for centuries. The first example here dates from around the beginning of the 10th century A.D. and is part of the Chinese Loh River scroll. Perfect magic squares must use consecutive numbers, each one only once, to produce the same total across each horizontal line and from corner to corner. Not only does The Loh River 15 achieve this but, by using beads instead of written numbers, the compiler of nearly 1000 years ago has brilliantly added an additional dimension to the puzzle by showing even numbers as black and odd numbers as white.

Over the years magic squares have acquired a reputation for occult and mystical properties and have been inscribed on charms to ward off evil spirits and bring good luck. The real charm of these squares, however, is the seemingly endless mathematical properties which they reveal and the number of different ways which they can be constructed. We have illustrated this with Five 5 X 5 Magic Squares.

During the seventeenth century, French mathematicians took the construction of magic squares further, and later, in the eighteenth century, the American diplomat, scientist and author Benjamin Franklin became one of the world's leading

64	57	4	5	56	49	12	13
3	6	63	58	11	14	55	50
61	60	1	8	53	52	9	16
2	7	62	59	10	15	54	51
48	41	20	21	40	33	28	29
19	22	47	42	27	30	39	34
45	44	17	24	37	36	25	32
18	23	46	43	26	31	38	35

3. The Frierson 260

30	39	48	1	10	19	28
38	47	7	9	18	27	29
46	6	8	17	26	35	37
5	14	16	25	34	36	45
13	15	24	33	42	44	4
21	23	32	41	43	3	12
22	31	40	49	2	11	20

4. The 7 X 7 Standard 175

authorities on magic squares (possibly as a result of his years spent as a diplomat in Paris) and devised new types of squares with intriguing patterns. In the second example here, devised by Franklin, all horizontal and vertical lines total 260, but alas, to purists it cannot be classed as a true magic square as the sums of the two corner-to-corner lines do not equal this total. However, more importantly, this square does introduce us to what is known as the property of bent diagonals and symmetrical patterns which produce the same magic total of 260. We leave you to discover as many of these patterns as you can (turn to Magic Square Introduction 1 when you think you have exhausted all possibilities).

A century after Franklin, in England, another magic square guru, Dr. Frierson, was able to improve the Franklin 260 by devising the mind-blowing square in the third example. Not only do all horizontal, vertical and comer-to-corner lines total 260, as demanded by the purists, but again there are many symmetrical patterns for you to discover (see Magic Square Introduction 2). In addition, there is a further startling property whereby the whole divides into four 4 X 4 magic squares, each adding up to 130.

Before leaving you to tackle the kaleidoscope of magic square puzzles which follows, here are a few hints which will enable you to construct at least one magic square for every odd number from 3 X 3 upwards.

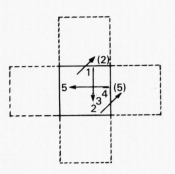

Taking, for example, the 7 X 7 square shown in the fourth example, the system of construction holds good for any odd number. It is simply to start at the middle square of the top row and move diagonally upwards (imagine four squares reproduced adjacent to the sides of the main square and move into them; the numbers reappear in the same position in the main square–see the fifth example, left).

When you reach the top of a line, you go to the bottom of the next line to the right: for example, from 1 to 2. When you reach the end of a line, you go to the beginning of the line above; for example, from 45 to 46. When you reach the top right-hand-corner square, you go to the square below: for example, from 28 to 29. The only other move is when your upward diagonal path is blocked by another number, in which case you go to the square directly below: for example, from 35 to 36.

Easy when you know how!

Five 5 x 5 Magic Squares

It is possible to arrange the numbers 1 to 25 in several ways to form a magic square where each horizontal, vertical and corner-to-corner line totals 6. Can you insert the numbers 1 to 25 in each of the grids below to find five different 5 x 5 magic squares? In each square two of the numbers are already positioned and your task is to insert the remaining numbers correctly.

(a)

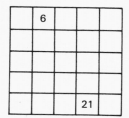

(b)

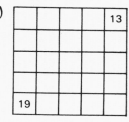

(c)

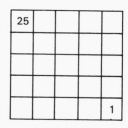

(d)

(e)

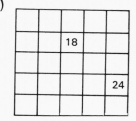

The Magic Nine Square

When the sum of the digits of a number will divide exactly by nine, then the number itself will also divide by nine: for example, 2673 and 2 + 6 + 7 + 3 = 18. With this in mind, place the digits into the grid so that each horizontal, vertical and corner-to-corner line, when read both forwards and backwards, will divide exactly by nine, and also the sum of the four corner numbers will divide by nine.

1, 1, 1
2, 2, 2
3, 3
4, 4, 4, 4
5, 5, 5
6, 6, 6
7, 7, 7, 7
8, 8
9

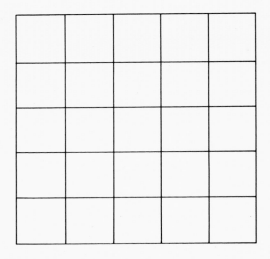

Magic Square Jigsaw Puzzle

Insert the sections into the grid to form a 10 X 10 magic square so that each horizontal, vertical and corner-to-corner line totals 505.

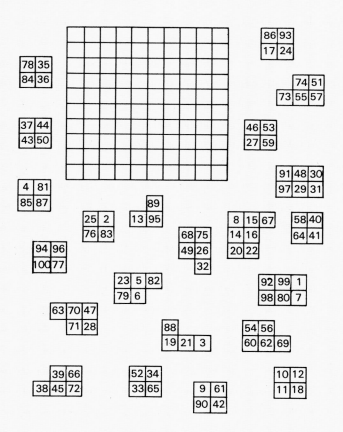

Magic Square 1

Fill the grid with the numbers 1 to 16 to form a magic square so that each horizontal, vertical and corner-to-corner line totals 34. One number is already inserted.

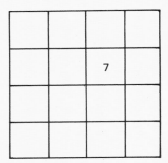

		7	

The Incredible Square!

Here is a magic square in which all horizontal, vertical and corner-to-corner lines add up to 264. What is most unusual about it?

96	11	89	68
88	69	91	16
61	86	18	99
19	98	66	81

Magic Hexagon

Arrange the numbers 1 to 19 so that all connected straight lines (that is, horizontals and diagonals) add up to the same total.

For example: A + B + C = B + E + I + M

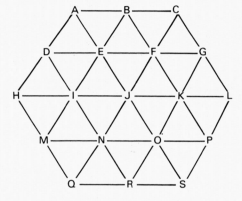

Eight-Pointed Star

Distribute the numbers 1 to 16 around the nodes so that
each of the eight lines adds up to the same number.

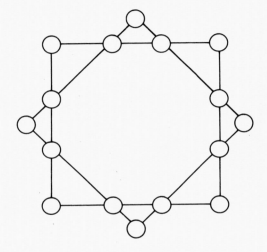

KICKSELF

Kickself puzzles, the ones which usually have an "obvious when you know it" answer, are well known in Mensa circles. Here are some typical examples. What was the first human artefact to break the sound barrier? (Kickself Introduction of Intelligence Challengers). Why are round manhole covers safer than square manhole covers? (Kickself Introduction of Intelligence Challengers 2). On a building site some workmen tell their foreman they have just found a coin marked 10 B.C.; why does the foreman suddenly realize they must be pulling his leg? (Kickself Introduction of Intelligence Challengers 3). Why are 1989 coins worth more than 1988 coins? (Kickself Introduction of Intelligence Challengers 4). A woman has borne just two sons, which she gave birth to on the same day at 30-minute intervals; they are identical, but not twins. What is the explanation? (Kickself Introduction of Intelligence Challengers 5).

Each month a kickself puzzle appears in *Mensa*, the journal of British Mensa, with a prize for the first correct solution drawn out. We are usually inundated with correct entries, but occasionally one puzzle appears which seems, for whatever reason, to stump almost everyone. Before leaving you to tackle our following compilation of kickself puzzles, here is one which was solved by only a handful of people when it appeared in *Mensa* in April 1987. (Kickself Introduction of Intelligence Challengers 6)

In Oxford Street, London, I saw one of these new-fangled buses. One cannot tell the front from the rear and, when stationary, in which direction the bus is heading. Which way is the bus heading: A or B?

Signpost

A traveller in a strange country, with no map, comes to a crossroads where a signpost has been knocked down. How can he find his way without asking anyone for directions?

Unique Number

What is unique about the number 854,917,632?

Ceremonial Sword

On Japanese trains there is a rule that forbids passengers bringing on to the train objects longer than 36 inches. How did a passenger travel with a ceremonial sword that was 42 inches long?

B.C./A.D.

A Greek was born on the 260th day of 20 B.C. and died on the 260th day of A.D. 60. How many years did he live?

Manhattan

In Manhattan the avenues run north to south and the streets run east to west. 11 friends who work at the intersection of the roads marked with an asterisk wish to meet on a street corner with the least possible amount of total walking distance. On which corner should they meet?

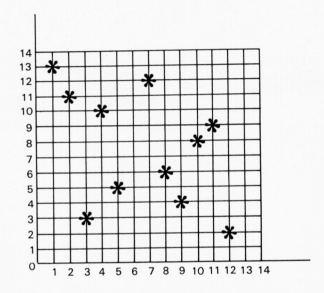

Water to Wine

A full cask of wine has a bung hole on the top surface. You have only a bottle full of water. Without moving the cask or damaging it, and using no other appliances, how can you obtain a bottle of wine from the cask?

Pantechnicon

The driver and his pantechnicon weigh 10 tons. His cargo of 200 uncaged sleeping pigeons weighs 200 lb. The driver approaches a 10-ton-limit bridge, stops, gets out, bangs on the side of the pantechnicon to make the pigeons fly about, gets back in and drives over the bridge safely. In practice his actions were correct because he managed to cross the bridge safely, but was his reasoning correct in theory?

Arabian Knight

An Arab came to the riverside,
With a donkey bearing an obelisk,
But he did not venture to ford the tide,
For he had too good an *.

* What is the missing word?

Series 2

Can you draw the next figure in this series?

Lunch at the Club

Every member of the Luncheon Club is either a truther, who always tells the truth when asked a question, or a liar, who always answers with a lie. When I visited the club for the first time, I found its members, all men, seated around a large circular table, having lunch. There was no way to distinguish truthers from liars by their appearance and so I asked each man in turn which he was. This proved unenlightening. Each man naturally assured me he was a truther. I tried again, this time asking each man whether his neighbor on the left was a truther or a liar. To my surprise each told me the man on his left was a liar. Later in the day, back home and typing up my notes on the luncheon, I discovered I had forgotten to record the number of men at the table. I telephoned the club's president. He told me the number was 37. After hanging up I realized that I could not be sure of this figure because I did not know whether the president was a truther or a liar. I then telephoned the club's secretary.

"No, no," the secretary said. "Our president, unfortunately, is an unmitigated liar. There were actually 40 men at the table."

Which man, if either, should I believe? Suddenly I saw a simple way to resolve the matter.

Was it 37 or 40?

CODES AND CIPHERS

Nothing seems to grip the public's imagination more than a treasure hunt. The Klondike Gold Rush of 1896 in America was a prime example and also, more recently in England, there was the occasion when an author buried some treasure and then published a book giving cryptic clues to its location and people enthusiastically combed the countryside for days looking for it. Incidentally, the treasure was never found.

Since 1845, in America, many people have devoted a great deal of their time to trying to break what is known as the Beale Cyphers in an attempt to find the whereabouts of several tons of gold, silver and jewels supposedly buried near the town of Montvale (formally Bufords), Virginia. It was a Virginian, Thomas J. Beale, who set out with a party of men in 1817 on a hunting trip which eventually took them towards the Colorado mountains. Here they discovered gold and stayed on to mine both gold and silver for 18 months. Then in November 1819, fearing for their safety and their vast fortune, they returned to Virginia to hide their treasure in a secret excavation six feet below ground. Two years later they again returned to the site with some $13,000 in jewels, which they had purchased in St Louis. During this time Tom Beale had become acquainted with Robert Morriss, the proprietor of a hotel where he stayed, and he entrusted to Morriss a strong iron box for safekeeping. Later he wrote to Morriss, asking him to keep the box for 10 years and telling him that if he had not by then called to collect it, to open it up. Beale was never heard of again, but to be on the safe side Morriss waited for almost 25 years before finally opening the box in 1845. Inside he found several sheets of paper and letters telling the story of the treasure, together with three cryptograms, or ciphers, giving details of the location of the treasure, its contents and Beale's next of kin. One letter promised that the three ciphers could easily be cracked using a key which would be sent to Morriss, but it never arrived. As Morriss could not crack the ciphers he enlisted the help of a friend, who became obsessed with them and after some 20 years was finally able to crack one of the ciphers, the one giving the contents of the vault of treasure.

The method which he discovered Beale had used was to take the Declaration of Independence and allocate each word a number, from WHEN = 1 to HONOR = 1322, then, taking the first letter of the word which corresponded to each number of the cipher, the message was spelled out, starting: 115(I), 73(H), 24(A), 807(V), 37(E), 52(D), 49(E), 17(P), 31(O), 62(S), 647(I), 22(T)

Since then, the remaining two ciphers have remained a mystery, despite many thousands of hours of research and effort, and no treasure has been found. Whether the Beale treasure is genuine or a hoax we cannot be sure, but research is still continued, especially by the members of the Beale Cypher Association in Pennsylvania.

No story could better illustrate the appeal of codes and ciphers. The handful of puzzles which follows contains some original codes and ciphers of our own invention. We cannot promise you any buried treasure, but hopefully you will spend some entertaining minutes or hours solving them, and for any that you cannot crack, at least you will not have to wait years for the answer, as all you have to do is turn to the back of the book!

Coded Message

Decode the following to reveal a message:

ECHO, MOOD, LIMA, SIERRA, SOUND, PAPA, BEACH, TANGO, IDEA, WHISKY, SCREEN, QUEEN, ROMEO, MAE, WEST, CROON, CHAMPAGNE, QUEST, WROTE, FOIL, IMMORTAL, FIELDS.

Cryptosymbol 1

Decode the following:

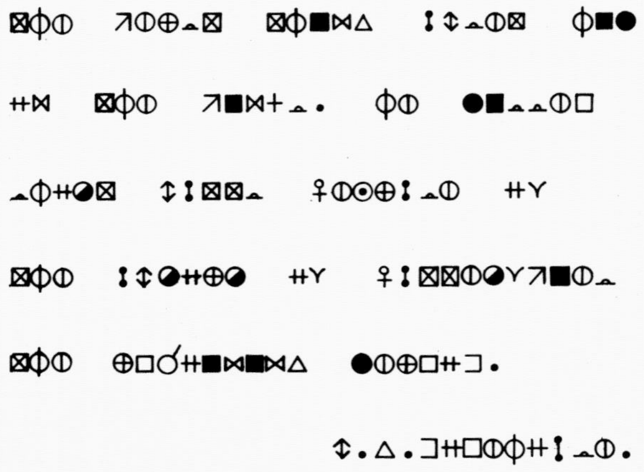

Carter Cipher

Decode the following:

686, 323, 311, 457, 010, 819, 001, 121, 663, 879, 324, 775, 100, 030, 777, 446, 18, 441, 239, 151, 011, 212, 010, 784, 488

Cryptograms

Each cryptogram is a straight substitution code where every letter of the alphabet has been replaced by another. Each of the three is in a different code.

1. OE XYHSWSNH SN O WOE BRX NHOJHN O MJXNNBXJZ YPFFCD BSHR O IXPEHOSE YDE.

2. XNW YOH ENG DYPFWD ENWH XNPHZD ZG ETGHZ NOD XNGMZNX GA DGYWGHW NW SOH KFOYW PX GH.

   —BGHWD' FOE

3. VT FHTHYUN, BAH UYB JQ FJXHYTDHTB IJTRVRBR VT BUCVTF UR DKIA DJTHO UR ZJRRVLNH QYJD-JTH ZUYBOJQBAH IVBVPHTR BJ FVXH BJ BAH JBAHY.

   —XJNBUYYH

CROSSWORD VARIATIONS

1988 was not only the year in which the 75th anniversary of the publication of the first-ever crossword puzzle was celebrated; it was also the year in which a milestone was reached for one of the authors of this book, being the 50th year after the young Kenneth Russell began his interest in compiling crosswords. As a pupil of the Strand Grammar School in Tulse Hill, South London, he was among a small group of boys who assisted the headmaster, L. S. Dawe, in compiling the *Daily Telegraph* crossword.

Some years after this, in 1945, Mr. Dawe was still compiling the *Telegraph* crossword, with another group of boys, when, shortly before the D-day invasion of France by the Allies in the Second World War, he received a visit from MI and was detained for questioning because one edition of the newspaper contained the following crossword answers: Fido, Pluto, Omaha and Overlord. All were key code names used in the invasion plans. Mr. Dawe somehow convinced MI that this was just coincidence. However, it was not until 1980 that the mystery was finally unravelled when a letter appeared in the *Sunday Times* from an old boy of the school who had been a member of the crossword team. He confessed to having been the culprit. It appeared that his mother had been evacuated to Lincolnshire during the war and had found work in an American Air Force base. He frequently visited her on weekends and moved freely about the camp, where these secret code names were often bandied about. The names had stuck with him and he had, as a result, fed them into the crossword grid.

Ken's interest in crosswords has never waned since those traumatic times of half a century ago, and together we have devised the following selection of variations on the traditional crossword theme. We start with our tribute to the world's first-ever cruciverbalist (crossword constructor), Liverpool-born Arthur Wynne, whom we have to thank for his invention of 77 years ago.

Wynne's Winner

The grid below is the exact design used by Arthur Wynne when he compiled the first crossword puzzle, which appeared in the *New York World* on Sunday 21 December 1913. Called a word-cross puzzle, it is reproduced here with a completely new set of clues and answers.

CLUES:

Across

2. Piece of timber (3)
4. Passageway in theater (5)
6. Seriously thoughtful (7)
8. Type of footwear (4)
9. Waist band (4)
11. Mild expletive (4)
12. Want (4)
14. Garrison (4)

15. Grasp (4)
16. Hard work (4)
18. Hard grating noise (4)
19. Christmas (4)
21. Eat dinner (4)
22. Closest at hand (7)
24. Rap sharply (5)
25. Large deer (3)

Down

1. Low tufted plant (4)
2. Fabric with raised nap (4)
3. Fluently insincere (4)
4. Long period of time (4)
5. Not odd (4)
6. Part of a whole (7)
7. Dignified and graceful (7)
8. Member of nobility (5)
10. Neatly brief and concise (5)

11. Small round mark (3)
13. Plunge (3)
17. National emblem of Wales (4)
18. Expose to danger (4)
20. Narrow road (4)
21. Ship's platform (4)
23. Turn over and over (4)

Jig Word

Place the x sets in the grid to complete the crossword.

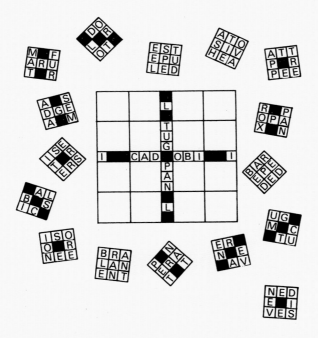

Cross-Alphabet 1

Insert the 26 letters of the alphabet into the grid, using each one only once, to form a crossword. The clues are in no particular order.

CLUES:

Defensive players
Trot along
Behind the true time
The west wind
Exasperate
Express amount of Indistinct

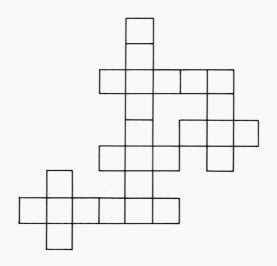

Nursery Rhyme Crossword 2

There was a crooked man who walked a crooked mile. He found some crooked silver pieces which had fallen out of the crooked pocket of a crooked man in charge of a crooked football match by a crooked stile. With the crooked money he bought crooked mice and a crooked snake and they all lived together with twin girls in a crooked house and he puts up with the racket which sounds louder each day.

Find the eight clues, solve them and place the answers in the grid.

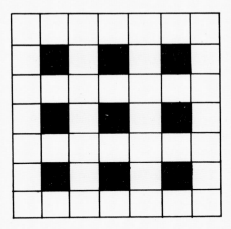

Word Power

The answers to the clues are to be found in the grid in letter order.

They are all nine-letter words. For example: Deciduous.

CLUES:

1. Shedding leaves
2. Small underground burrowing creature
3. Exaggerated statement
4. Greatness
5. Reclining
6. Trite saying
7. Narrow-minded
8. Sweetmeat
9. Simple covering for lower middle part of body

H	L	R	L	D	H	E	W	M
E	O	Y	E	I	I	A	A	I
D	I	G	R	T	C	Q	P	C
I	N	T	N	T	E	U	U	E
I	B	C	H	I	M	O	R	D
C	U	B	T	B	L	W	R	O
O	E	O	O	I	O	U	I	U
L	T	U	S	N	D	N	R	C
H	E	S	M	M	T	E	D	E

"A" Frame

Each horizontal and vertical line indicates the consonants of a word which can be completed by adding a number of A vowels. The two-figure number at the end of each line indicates the number of consonants and A vowels: for example, 3-2 indicates three consonants and two A vowels. Each letter in the grid is used once only and all letters must be used. The consonants to be used in each line are not necessarily in the correct order or adjacent.

CLUES:

Across

1. Trite
2. Hoax
3. Danger
4. Eastern native
5. Coward
6. Gather
7. Indian sailor

Down

1. Pineapple
2. Chasm
3. Certain
4. Waterway
5. Structures
6. White ball in bowls
7. Parrot

	1	2	3	4	5	6	7	
1	L	S	T	B	S	N	W	3-2
2	S	N	R	N	C	J	D	4-2
3	H	S	Z	L	D	R	C	4-2
4	B	Y	D	C	W	K	R	2-2
5	T	B	D	D	L	S	R	5-2
6	N	M	N	S	L	S	M	3-2
7	N	L	M	C	R	C	S	4-2
	3-3	4-1	4-3	3-2	4-1	3-1	3-2	

Select a Crossword

Each number has a choice of possible letters, as shown in the key. Select the correct letter for each square to form eight seven-letter interlocking words.

1	1	6	2	2	6	7
5		2		5		9
5	1	7	3	8	2	7
3		3		3		7
2	5	6	3	5	5	2
2		2		7		5
6	2	7	3	7	7	7

KEY:

1	A	B	C
2	D	E	F
3	G	H	I
4	J	K	L
5	M	N	O
6	P	Q	R
7	S	T	U
8	V	W	X
9	Y	Z	

DIY Crosswords

Place all the words below into the two empty grids to form two crossword puzzles.

NO	TAP	EON	RED	BETS	TOOL
ME	SPA	NIT	APT	ACHE	ERAS
IT	SHY	ANT	YET	EVEN	EMIT
SO	LAP	ROE	ACE	WETS	SLIP
TO	PUT	LAM	MOW	KNOW	SLAP
IN	SON	TEA	TOW	AIDE	SICK
AS	BIT	HEN	SAT	PETS	EDGY
IS	TEG	GET	ART	SPEW	TOIL

MOTET	DRAUGHT	APPEALING
NOTES	EPAULET	PRESCRIBE
SEDAN		CRINOLINE
SPENT		IMPRUDENT

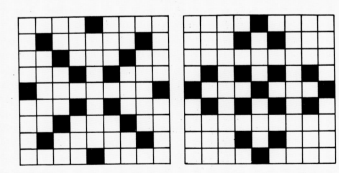

Clueless Cross Alphabet 1

Insert the 26 letters of the alphabet to complete the crossword.

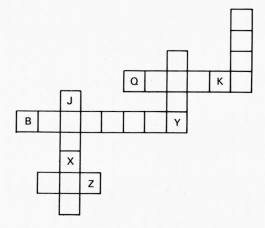

Seven of the letters have already been inserted.

A Ⓑ C D E F G
H I Ⓙ Ⓚ L M N
O P Ⓠ R S T U
V W Ⓧ Ⓨ Ⓩ

Clueless Crossword 1

In each square there are four letters. Your task is to cross out three of each four, leaving one letter in each square, so that the crossword is made up in the usual way with good English interlocking words.

T A	X O	S N	D A	A Q	A R	F D
E C	R A	E P	N C	E B	D O	Y T
A B		I A		X A		A H
R O		R H		V U		R I
E W	E V	Z E	A E	U A	G I	Y N
A O	G J	I T	R P	I T	A N	E G
I M		F D		T E		E A
L S		O C		D U		H R
O E	X R	L N	I E	Q E	M X	N T
P J	C B	F E	T L	T L	U B	E D

BRAINBENDERS

In this section we present a diverse collection of puzzles which have just one thing in common—their high degree of difficulty.

Bath

The plumber left the taps running in the bath with the plug out. The hot water tap on would fill the bath in 54 seconds. The cold water tap on would fill the bath in 48 seconds. The plug out would release a bath full of water in 30 seconds. Would the bath ever fill up?

Missing Sum

The addition sum below is written out in a very unusual way. Try to work out the logic to decipher the figures and arrive at the correct answer.

$$7|\ \sqsubset| + |\ ''| \sqsubset$$

$$= ?$$

Brain Strain 1

Insert numbers into the remaining blank squares so that all the calculations are correct reading both across and down.

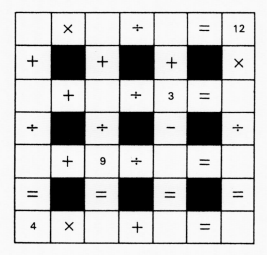

Dodecahedra

I have an indefinite number of regular dodecahedra, indistinguishable in appearance from each other. I have pots of red and blue paint. If each face of each dodecahedron is to be painted red or blue, how many dodecahedra that are distinguishable from one another shall I be able to produce?

Dodecahedron: a solid figure having twelve plane faces.

Food for Thought

When the following numbers are applied to malt

160934.4

.4046873

33.81402

2240.0

what is malt converted to?

Law of the Search

Start at the top left-hand square and work from square to square horizontally, vertically or diagonally to find the Law of the Search. Visit every square only once and finish at the bottom right-hand square.

T	H	H	E	L	A	A	C
F	E	T	T	S	L	Y	E
L	I	R	S	P	W	U	O
A	P	T	S	I	G	O	U
O	C	E	I	N	P	L	D
L	T	T	H	E	C	X	E
O	K	F	Y	T	T	T	O
O	O	R	A	N	I	B	E

Helpuselph

A settler in the island of Helpuselph applied to the Governor for some land.

"How much would you like?" asked the Governor.

"About 100 square miles."

"OK," said the Governor. "You may choose a rectangular parcel of land in the township of Little Rainfall. Its dimensions must be such that if one side of the rectangle were 5 miles longer, and the other 4 miles longer, the area of the rectangle would be twice as great, and its perimeter must be exactly 46 miles."

The applicant duly selected and fenced his land in accordance with these conditions. But he got away with 6 square miles more than the Governor had anticipated. What was the area of the selected rectangle?

Cubes

Express 100 as the sum of three cubes, allowing each cube to be positive or negative. There are only three known answers, one of which is:

$$190^3 - 161^3 - 139^3$$

Can you find the other two solutions, one with larger numbers and one with smaller numbers than the solution above?

Clueless Cross Alphabet 2

Insert the 26 letters of the alphabet to complete the crossword. Four of the letters have already been inserted.

A B C D E F G H I J (K) L M
N O (P) Q R S T U V W (X) Y (Z)

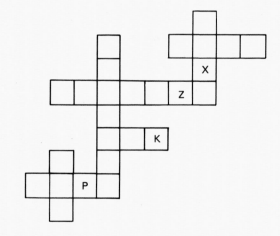

Triangles 3

The largest number of non-overlapping triangles that can be produced by drawing seven straight lines is 11. Your task below is to work out how this can be done. Three lines are already in position, showing just one triangle, and you must add a further four straight lines to the figure to produce the 11 non-overlapping triangles.

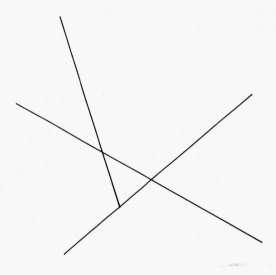

RUSSELL SQUARES

R	O	T	A	S
O	P	E	R	A
T	E	N	E	T
A	R	E	P	O
S	A	T	O	R

Magic word squares, like magic number squares, have their own special fascination. The famous example on the left is believed to have been engraved on a piece of wall plaster in Roman times and was discovered in 1868 at Cirencester, where it is now exhibited at the Corinium Museum. It is unique because the words read the same not only across and down, as with conventional magic squares, but also backwards and upwards! Never since has anyone, in any language, achieved a magic word square with these properties.

Magic word squares become progressively more difficult to compile as the number of words increases. Several 8 x 8 squares have been achieved and there have been many attempts at nine- and ten-letter squares but, regretfully, these have either contained words for which meanings cannot be found or repeated words and tautonyms (words consisting of repeated words: for example, Baden-Baden). So the challenge is still there to compile a nine- or ten-letter word square consisting of different words with known meanings, a challenge which was, incidentally, issued some three years ago in the British Mensa journal—but no solution was ever received.

Two 5 X 5 Magic Squares

The answers to the clues, which are in no particular order, are all five-letter words. When the answers are placed in the correct position in the correct grid, two magic squares will be formed so that the same five words can be read both across and down.

CLUES:

Pendent fleshy part of soft palate
Angry
Authorized
Firm
Former gold coin of Italy
Exhilarate
Valleys
Valued
More vulgar
Work of music

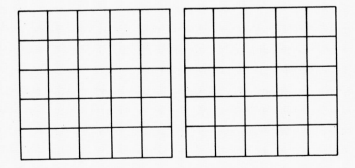

Two 6 X 6 Magic Squares

The answers to the clues, which are in no particular order, are all six-letter words. When the answers are placed in the correct position in the correct grid, two magic squares will be formed so that the same six words can be read both across and down.

CLUES:

Drink
Participates
Natural ability
Reach
Buy back
Strike continuously
More emotionally strained
Pared away
Develop gradually
Large piece of landed property
Disinclined
Three-legged stand

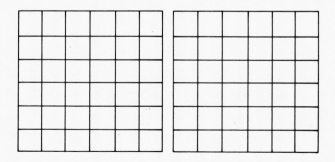

Clueless Magic Squares

(a) Insert the 40 letters below into the remaining spaces in the grids to form two 5 X 5 magic squares so that in each grid the same words can be read both across and down.

A, A, A, E, E, E, E, E, E, F, F, H, I, L, L, N, N, O, O, P, P, P, P, R, R, R, R, R, R, S, S, S, S, S, T, T, T, T, W, W

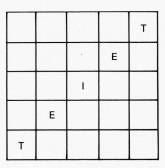

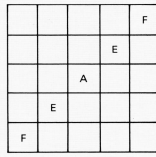

(b) Rearrange the letters to form a magic square where the five words read the same both across and down.

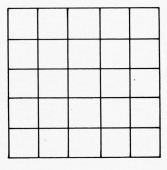

ET CETERA

Next, when you are describing,
A shape, or sound, or tint;
Don't state the matter plainly,
But put it in a hint;
And learn to look at all things,
With a sort of mental squint.
                    —*Lewis Carroll*

For this section we have chosen another miscellany of puzzles to test and tease you. We hope you have enjoyed the selection of brainteasers that we have presented you with and that you have been successful in coming up with many of the correct solutions.

Zoetrope

When the zoetrope* has been spun into the position below, the word ORB on the outer circle gives the word RUE on the inner circle: this is done by taking the letters O-R-B on the outer circle, then finding their corresponding letters, R-U-E, in the same order on the inner circle.

Using this system with the zoetrope in the same position, find another three-letter word in the outer circle which will also give a three-letter word in the inner circle. Then find a four-letter word. Then find the five-letter name of a reptile on the outer circle which spells out the name of a famous Austrian on the inner circle.

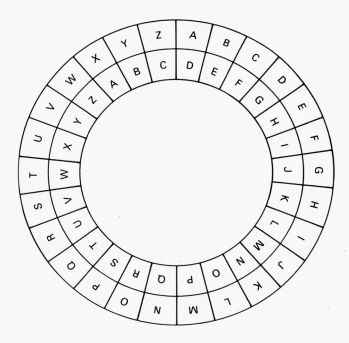

*Zoetrope: A toy with a revolving cylinder which shows a series of pictures as if the subject were alive and moving.

Double Acrostic

Each couplet provides the clue to a word. Solve the clues and list the six words. Two more words will be spelled out by the first and last letters of the six words.

A tiny note, it's in quick time,
All you need to solve this rhyme?

Cry to Mark, it's so abrupt,
Delight or horror will erupt.

Set a course to steer the ship,
Plot the route when off you trip.

Just a drop to come apart,
Joy perhaps, or sad at heart?

Describe a lad who now is striving,
One day his hopes may be arriving.

Sculpture of freedom and all is well,
Here's independence and the marching bell.

Early Arrival

My wife usually leaves work at 4:30 p.m., stops at the supermarket, then catches the 5 p.m. train, which arrives at our home town station at 5:30 p.m. I leave home each day, drive to the station and pick up my wife at 5:30 p.m., just as she gets off the train. One day last week my wife was able to finish work about five minutes earlier than usual, decided to go straight to the station instead of stopping at the supermarket and managed to catch the 4:30 p.m. train, which arrived at our home town station at 5 p.m. Because I was not there to pick her up she began to walk home. I left home at the usual time, saw my wife walking, turned around, picked her up and drove home, arriving there 12 minutes earlier than usual. For how long did my wife walk before I picked her up?

Chess Tournament

At an international chess tournament the four semi-finalists, Zena Le Vue, Dr. A. Glebe, Rob E. Lumen and Ann Ziata, each represented one of four continents: Europe, Africa, the Americas and Australasia. Can you correctly match each of the four chess masters with the continent which they represented?

Common Clues 1

What do the answers to the following clues all have in common?

Tract of waste land
Dwelling place
Place of great delight or contentment
A rule
Flake off
Ashen
A cardinal point

Categorize 1

Arrange the following into groups of three:

AMITY
  ASTRONOMY
    CONCORD
      COMET
        CHEMISTRY
          DOUGLAS
            HARMONY
              HARRIER
                PEACE
                  PLANET
                    PHYSICS
                      STAR

Color Problem

On a map showing country boundaries, what is the least number of colors required to color in the map so that adjoining countries have different colors?

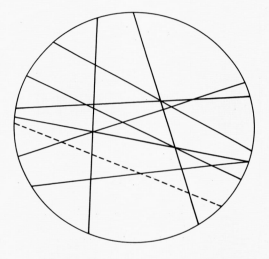

Where countries join at a point they are not considered to be adjoining.

How many colors are required if an additional boundary (shown dotted) is added?

Groups

Find 29 names given to groups of animals, birds, fish and objects hidden in the following three paragraphs.

In the cove near Hove rafters tend to rake and span and slot home on buildings.

In the same cove your outer charm will be the downfall of a gang of husky gamblers.

You can hear the snide remarks of a wisp of blushing kennel maids as they drift and clamor and mingle and hover and cry at the observance of a dray full of troops.

Triplicities

What letters should replace the question marks below?

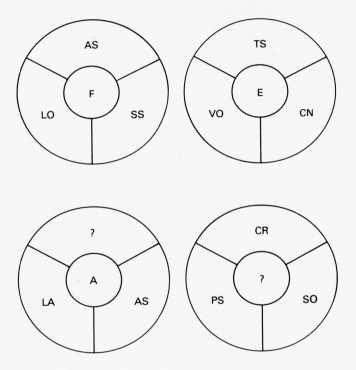

Arms

Find the missing square.

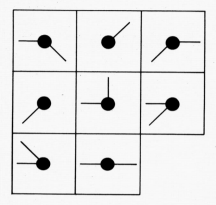

Choose from:

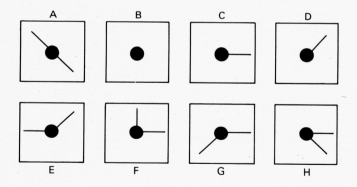

A B C D

E F G H

Names Riddle

Last week it was the 70th birthday party of my uncle. It was good to meet up with some of my relatives again, particularly my brother, Bert, and sister-in-law, Lena. Auntie Tina put on a splendid buffet supper with the help of my half-cousin Flo, and at the end of the evening we had the pleasure of drinking a toast to the health of my uncle. What is his name?

Coup de Grace

Five friends, Andrew, Bernard, Claude, Donald and Eugene, each have a son and a daughter. Their families are so close that each has married his daughter to the son of one of his friends, and as a result the daughter-in-law of the father of Andrew's son-in-law is the sister-in-law of Bernard's son, and the son-in-law of the father of Claude's daughter-in-law is the brother-in-law of Donald's daughter.

But although the daughter-in-law of the father of Bernard's daughter-in-law has the same mother-in-law as the son-in-law of the father of Donald's son-in-law, the situation is simplified by the fact that no daughter-in-law is the sister-in-law of the daughter of her father-in-law. Who married Eugene's daughter?

Mind Bafflers

WARM-UPS

The first part of this section is a puzzle pot pourri to prepare your mind for what is to follow and perhaps to give you some insight into the ways our minds work. It is also meant to give your mind a break from the previous puzzles that may have challenged your intelligence before tackling another set of baffling brainteasers. All of the puzzles are compiled in the spirit of fun and are meant to be a leisurely diversion from life's more pressing problems. Good luck, happy solving, and have fun!

Letter Sequences 1

1. What is the next letter in the sequence
   F,S,T,F?

2. What letter completes the sequence
   S, O, E, N, S, Y?

3. What is next in the sequence
   A,B,G,D,E?

4. What is the next letter in the sequence
   C, B, R, R, C ?

5. What is the next letter in the sequence
   F, A, J, N, S, A, D, J?

Keywords

1. I am eight letters long – 12345678.
My 1234 is an atmospheric condition.
My 34567 supports a plant.
My 4567 is to appropriate.
My 45 is a friendly thank-you.
My 678 is a canny name.

What am I?

2. I am seven letters long – 1234567.
My 123 is a vehicle.
My 2345 was a pop group.
My 456 is a piece of luggage.
My 567 is a period of time.

What am I?

3. I am nine letters long – 123456789.
My 123 is a mischief.
My 3456 is to the left.
My 678 is a shade of brown.
My 789 is a social insect.

What am I?

The Knight's Tour

Find the correct starting point and then, by the knight's tour, spell out the message. The knight moves as in chess – see diagram below.

BE	ARE	OF	FUN	TEASERS
SIMPLE	MUCH	CAN	COMING	SOLVING
PEOPLE	IN	REALIZE	MATHS	THERE
HOW	LITTLE	MORE	THE	TO

Letters

Where would you insert the letters D and K in the grid?

G	M		J
B	L	E	O
I	C	N	H
P	F		A

Four Teasers

1. "How much is this bag of potatoes?" asked the man. "32lb divided by half its own weight," said the shop-keeper. How much did the bag of potatoes weigh?

2. A workman was repairing telephone boxes that had been vandalized in the town center. The chief engineer said: "See those 12 boxes in a line over there? Well, seven out of the first nine are broken. Go and mend one of them." The workman went straight to number nine. How did he know that one was broken?

3. A tramp collected cigarette ends until he had 1728. How many cigarettes in total could he make and smoke from these if 12 cigarette ends make up one cig-arette?

4. What is the next letter in the sequence D, H, M, S?

Riddle

You are looking for a one-word answer to this riddle.

Leave the tea and get me a pot,
And I'll devise a devious plot.
Ideas are fixed firmly in my mind,
As I lay in my bed, my thoughts entwined,
I cannot sleep, so I take a drink,
Breathe in the air, I'm on the brink.
This story will be the best seller yet,
The sweet smell of success I'll surely get.

Logic 2

Use logical deduction to determine which letter should replace the question mark.

Find the Number

Find the correct starting point and work from square to square, horizontally, vertically and diagonally, to spell out a number. The letters that are not used can be arranged to form the Roman numeral value of the number spelled out.

L	H	E	U	H	M
U	N	S	X	O	T
N	N	I	A	O	Y
D	D	N	W	T	M
D	R	N	D	T	R
E	A	C	F	O	M

Letter Change

Change one letter from each word in every group to make, in each case, a well-known phrase. For example, Pet rice quack will become Get rich quick.

1. Bust she joy

2. Run any dames

3. Is lull dry

4. So life I dread

5. Rub sings bound

6. Toots any sail

7. Slow hit end cord

8. Plan in works

9. Hike any seem

10. Plan wits fine

11. Tame if mood tart

12. Bum o dead jar

13. Same toesay

14. Odd gives take

15. Wish oven army

16. On she ran

17. Put on older

18. Life end lot five

19. Let I love in

20. And odd cow

ODD ONE OUT

In the puzzles in this section your task is to find one good reason, over and above all others, why one of the options given is the odd one out. You will have to put your mind to work to explore all the possibilities and use a great deal of lateral thinking.

To try to give you some inkling into the way our minds work on this type of puzzle, we have devised the unusual example illustrated here, which we call "added difficulty." In

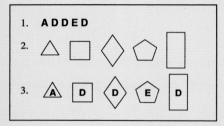

part 1, of the five letters shown—A, D, D, E and D—which is the odd one out? Our answer is A because it has lateral symmetry. In other words, if a line were drawn down the center from top to bottom the left side of the letter would be identical to the right side. The other letters have vertical symmetry—i.e., a line drawn across the middle from left to right will reveal identical top and bottom halves.

In part 2 the odd one out is the far right-hand figure (the rectangle) because all the other figures have identical sides.

The real difficulty begins in part 3. Which is the odd one out here? The reason cannot be the same as in parts 1 and 2. It cannot be argued that the figure containing the letter A is the odd one out because the letter A is laterally symmetrical, because you could equally argue that the last figure is the odd one out because its sides are unequal. If one of these figures is still the odd one out, it has to be because of something entirely different involving the marriage of letter and figure.

Can you work out the logic and discover which of the five figures is the odd one out? (See Odd One Out Introduction of Mind Bafflers.)

Find the Lady

Who is the odd one out—Diana, Mary, Deirdre or Carol?

Nine-Letter Words

Which is the odd one out?

Telephone
Limosine
Freighter
Driftwood

Nonsense Sentences

Which of the following nonsense phrases is the odd one out?

1. More solo goals

2. Lame animal pairs

3. Only some sail

4. Plaza mail louse

Odd One Out 3

Which is the odd one out?

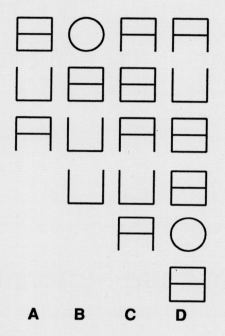

A B C D

Letters and Numerals

Which is the odd one out?

5OYN1O
100E500AR
E5OAN500
100AME5O
5050A1000A
BU5050

Odd One Out 4

Which is the odd one out?

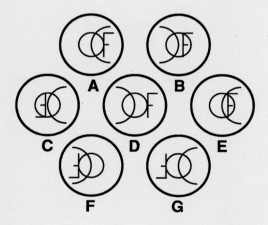

CRYPTOGRAPHY

Cryptography is the system of writing messages in codes or ciphers. A cryptogram is the coded message, and cryptanalysis is the breaking of the codes or cipher without the key.

The simplest cryptograms are those in which each letter of the alphabet from A to Z (the plain text) is substituted for another in the coded text; for example, F for H or B for T.

Another method is to substitute randomly chosen numbers for each letter—for example, 56 may stand for E or 29 for K. In even more complicated versions of such ciphers one letter may have more than one number equivalent—for example, the letter E may be 29 the first time it appears, 36 the second time and 21 the third time. These alternative numbers are known as homophones. Without the key such messages, and even more complicated variations of them, would be virtually impossible to decode except by intelligence departments with sophisticated equipment.

In this section we include several different types of cryptogram that have been developed throughout history, each of which will present its own demanding challenge.

The Polybius Cipher

This code is based on a cipher invented by a Greek writer, Polybius, in the second century B.C. Can you work out the system and decipher the quotation below?

```
A B C D E
F G H IJ K
L M N O P
Q R S T U
V W X Y Z
```

44,23,15   52,34,42,31,14,43
22,42,15,11,44   32,15,33
23,11,51,15   33,34,44
13,34,32,32,34,33,31,54
12,15,15,33   22,42,15,11,44
43,13,23,34,31,11,42,43   33,34,42
24,44,43   22,42,15,11,44
43,13,23,34,31,11,42,43
22,42,15,11,44   32,15,33

34,41,24,51,15,42
52,15,33,14,15,31,31
23,34,31,32,15,43

The Caesar Alphabet

This simple code was used by Julius Caesar when writing secret messages to his allies. Can you crack the system and decode the quotation?

YJJ   ZYB   NPCACBCLRQ   ZCEYL
YQ   HSQRGDGYZJC   KCYQSPCQ

Three-Letter Words

The Greek philosopher Pythagoras described three as the perfect number—it has a beginning, a middle and an end. The three-letter words below hide a familiar saying. Can you crack the code to reveal the saying?

mob	foe
log	toy
car	oil
ego	sun
ape	ear
fro	emu
wee	ill
beg	hub
jar	our
tap	awe

The Hidden Message

Can you find a hidden message in the memo below?

James is insisting that the second key to the office sup-plies cabinet, and the two colored transparencies, will first need clearance before Kenneth and Philip arrive at the office to check all the material early next Monday, so that Peter can develop them on Tuesday afternoon and take them around to David's department on Wednesday morning.

James is insisting that
the second key to the
office supplies cabinet,
and the two colored
transparencies, will
first need clearance
before Kenneth and
Philip arrive at the
office to check all the
material early next
Monday, so that Peter
can develop them on
Tuesday afternoon and
take them around to
David's department on
Wednesday morning.

Cryptosymbol 2

Decode the following quotation.

(encoded symbol text)

Three Cryptograms

Each cryptogram is a straight substitution code, where one letter of the alphabet has been replaced by another. Each of the three is in a different code. All three solutions are quotations.

1. O'A LCGS XCFF WNTRWOQPCZ PYY
XOPJ AWPPCGV AWPJCAWPONWF, O
RQZCGVPWQZ CTRWPOYQV, EYPJ PJC
VOAMFC WQZ TRWZGWPONWF.

                       X. V. UOFECGP

2. F VCRCRQCV QCFEJ MPETCT P
ZGNVC GNRXNZCT QU *RNDPV0 PO
OMC PJC NS CBCWCE. YMPO GNABT F
ZPU? F SCBO BFHC *TC *HNNEFEJ YMN
YPZ PZHCT ON GNRRCEO NE P
GCVOPFE PQZOVPGO XPFEOFEJ PET
PEZYCVCT FE OMC ECJPOFWC. MC YPZ
OMCE ON-BT FO YPZ OMC YNVH NS P
GCBCQVPOCT RNEHCU. 'OMPO'Z
TFSSCVCEO. SW P RNEHCU FO'Z
OCVVFSFG.'   FJNV ZOVPWFEZHU
(*indicates a capitalized word)

3. JN PJC VBOMUH GAACZUOYT XC
NRNZK FGY'H GUROAN ROMM JGRN G
AZCCDNU JCBHN. UGYOHJ SZCRNZV

Cryptokey 1

Start by solving the cryptogram that follows; it is a straightforward code in which each letter of the alphabet has been replaced by another.

FNHG LVNGK; N QOW'F, FSGD
QXHG IOKF OF KJQS
NZZGMJVOZ NWFGZAOVK

Now try to find a keyed phrase (6, 5) connected with the cryptogram. Against each letter of plain text (column 1) write its encoded form (column 2). Then, against each letter of code text (column 3) write its plain text form (column 4). You will find that some of column 4 is in alphabetical order; the letters that are not are those making up the key phrase. They appear in their correct order, but, of course, repeated letters have been omitted and must be replaced. A little imagination is needed to work out the hidden phrase—for instance, ANPLEDY would be all that would appear of "an apple a day."

	1	2	3	4	
A					A
B					B
C					C
D					D
E					E
F					F
G					G
H					H
I					I
J					J
K					K
L					L
M					M
N					N
O					O
P					P
Q					Q
R					R
S					S
T					T
U					U
V					V
W					W
X					X
Y					Y
Z					Z

Cryptokey 2

Using the same rules as in Cryptokey 1, decode the following, then find a keyed phrase (5, 6, 3, 3).

SKTOT SGR WQTLS
RQWLMXOLSXRMO RV SKT
*TMWAXOK OCTLZXMW
NTBRPQLPXTO SKT
*UQXSXOK TBCXQT LMN
SKT *EMXSTN *OSLSTO,
GXAA KLFT SR UT ORBTGKLS
BXHTN EC SRWTSKTQ XM
ORBT RV SKTXQ LVVLXQO...
X NR MRS FXTG SKT
CQRPTOO GXSK LMI
BXOWXFXMWO. X PREAN
MRS OSRC XS XV X GXOKTN;
MR RMT PLM OSRC XS. AXZT
SKT *BXOOXOOXCCX, XS
YEOS ZTTCO QRAAXMW
LARMW. ATS XS QRAA. ATS
XS QRAA RM VEAA VARRN,
XMTHRQLUAT,
XQQTOXOSXUAT
UTMXWMLMS, SR UQRLNTQ
ALMNO LMN UTSSTQ NLIO.
           GXMOSRM PKEQPKXAA

(*indicates a capitalized word)

1	2	3	4
A		A	
B		B	
C		C	
D		D	
E		E	
F		F	
G		G	
H		H	
I		I	
J		J	
K		K	
L		L	
M		M	
N		N	
O		O	
P		P	
Q		Q	
R		R	
S		S	
T		T	
U		U	
V		V	
W		W	
X		X	
Y		Y	
Z		Z	

WORD GAMES

**Words are like leaves; and where they most abound,
Much fruit of sense beneath is rarely found.**

—Alexander Pope

To have mastery over words is to have in one's possession the ability to produce order out of chaos. To a certain extent a puzzle compiler is a creator of chaos and is throwing out a challenge to the solver to sort out the chaos and to restore order—in other words, to find the solution that has in some way been disguised.

All the puzzles in this section involve fmding words from the grids or clues provided, and each provides its own different type of challenge.

Synchronized Synonyms

Each grid contains the letters of eight eight-letter words. All the letters are in the correct order, and each letter is used once only. Each word in Grid A has a synonym in Grid B, and the letters of each of the eight pairs of synonyms are in exactly the same position in each grid. Clues to each pair of synonyms are given below the grids in no particular order.

Example—the answers to the clue Crack are the words Fracture in Grid A and Splinter in Grid B.

Clues:

Crack
Contemplate
August
Subterfuge
Foreword
Childish
Viable
Macabre

GRID A

M	J	A	F	P	I	D	R
E	(F)	E	R	A	R	M	E
T	A	S	(R)	P	E	D	U
F	(A)	O	D	I	I	V	I
E	A	B	S	F	(C)	U	(T)
N	L	M	(U)	T	I	A	B
C	L	T	I	(R)	I	L	E
E	E	L	E	E	N	(E)	G

GRID B

R	I	P	W	P	M	G	R
O	(S)	U	R	R	H	A	O
E	U	K	(P)	J	O	L	M
I	(L)	E	M	T	I	M	A
A	L	B	S	E	(I)	S	(N)
T	L	O	(T)	N	N	A	G
C	U	T	T	(E)	U	R	E
E	E	H	E	E	I	(R)	C

Jumble

Commencing always with the center letter A, spell out eight 11-letter words. You may travel in any direction—horizontal, vertical or diagonal—but each letter must be used only once.

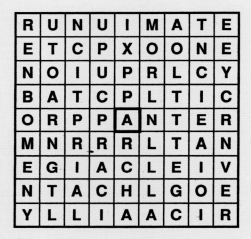

Square

Divide the square into four identical sections. Each section must contain the same nine letters, which can be arranged into a familiar nine-letter word.

H	L	U	B	A	E
E	L	A	G	G	A
B	B	U	L	L	A
A	A	A	U	H	L
U	L	G	A	E	B
H	L	G	E	H	L

Square Words

Work clockwise around the perimeter and finish at the center square to spell the six nine-letter words. You have to provide the missing letters. The six words you are looking for are three pairs of synonyms.

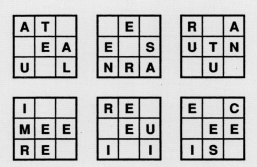

Pyramid Word

Solve the five clues, enter the correct words in the pyramid and then rearrange all the letters to find a 15-letter word.

The Roman numeral for 50 (1)
At home (2)
Came face to face (3)
Oxidation (4)
A person of exceptional holiness (5)

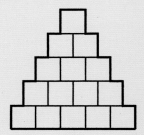

No-Repeat Letters

The grid contains 25 different letters. What is the longest word that can be found by starting anywhere and working from square to square, horizontally, vertically or diagonally, and not repeating a letter?

Y	K	C	H	V
P	M	L	I	G
J	O	A	U	N
B	F	R	Q	E
S	W	D	T	X

Word Construction 2

Use each of the 30 small words below once only to construct 10 words. There are three small words in each word.

IN	UP	POLL
FAT	DISC	OUT
BOUND	HER	ART
WARD	BAR	TRY
LEAGUE	FAN	CUE
KITCHEN	LAND	IF
ATE	OWL	IN
OUR	MEAD	SO
BE	RED	AGE
AND	ICE	BE

Pyramids

1. Spell out a 15-letter word by entering the pyramid one room at a time. Go into each room once only, but you may go into the passage as many times as you wish.

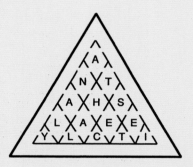

2. Spell out a 15-letter word by entering the pyramid one room at a time. Go into each room once only, but you may go into the passage as many times as you wish.

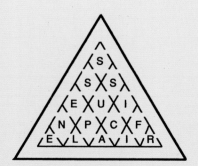

Hexagon

Fit the following words into the six spaces around the appropriate number on the diagram so that each word correctly interlinks with the two words on either side—you will see that each word has two consecutive letters in common with the word next to it.

Note: to arrive at the correct solution you will have to enter some words clockwise and some counterclockwise.

RECESS
REVOKE
SENSOR
REMOTE
DEVOUT
LANCER
SOLVED
TENDER
PLANET
ROUTED
TENNER
DETOUR

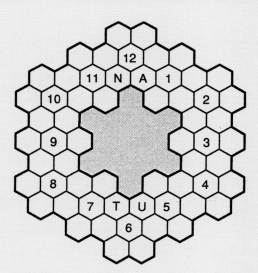

Categorize 2

Arrange the following words into four groups of three.

Barge	Beat
Hammer	Hike
Mark	Pound
Punt	Slog
Smack	Thrash
Tramp	Trek

Word Search

Hidden in the word square are 15 words that are rarely used in their positive form and that are better known in their negative form, usually when a prefix is placed in front of the positive word. See if you can find the 15 words. The words can be found in any direction, but always in a straight line.

For example, the clue Heedful would produce the answer Advertent which is the less often used positive form of the more commonly used negative form Inadvertent.

Positive-form clues:

1. Heedful
2. An agent of infection
3. Crystalline base affects allergic reactions
4. Correctable
5. Avoidable
6. An odorous substance
7. Comforted

8. Manageable
9. Free from weird qualities
10. Relating to life
11. Marked by finesse
12. Capable of being expressed
13. Trim
14. Allowable
15. Secure to a staff

E	N	I	M	A	T	S	I	H	T
L	V	E	L	B	A	F	F	E	N
B	T	I	Y	Y	L	T	T	H	A
I	P	B	T	D	N	A	N	T	T
G	M	L	I	A	L	N	I	U	C
I	E	O	R	O	B	E	A	O	E
R	K	O	S	U	T	L	I	C	F
R	D	N	O	R	F	I	E	W	N
O	O	L	I	C	I	T	C	A	I
C	T	N	E	T	R	E	V	D	A

KICKSELF

Lewis Carroll had a favorite trick that he enjoyed trying out on his friends. We have used the same trick many times. It never fails to amaze, and we have yet to find anyone who has worked out how it is done. We will take you through the trick stage by stage. First, you write a four-figure number on a piece of paper—for example, 3144 as shown—your "victim" is then invited to write another four-figure number underneath—for example, he or she may write down 7564. You then write another four-figure number beneath this—i.e., 2435. Next your "victim" writes down another number of his or her choice, in this case 3712, and you add the final number, 6287. Then the "victim" totals up the numbers to 23142, at which point you reach into your pocket, bring out a piece of paper folded and stapled and ask your "victim" to open it up. Needless to say, written on the paper is the number 23142.

Can you work out how this is done? It is a first class kickself puzzle. (See Kickself Introduction of Mind Bafflers)

$$
\begin{array}{r}
3144 \\
7564 \\
2435 \\
3712 \\
\underline{6287} \\
23142
\end{array}
$$

Equation

Correct the following equation by freely moving the given four digits but without adding any mathematical symbols.

26 = 47

Strike Out

Strike out 10 letters to reveal a short phrase.

ATSEHNLOERTPTHTREARSES

The Magic 11

Insert the 36 numbers into the grid in such a way that the same number does not appear in any horizontal or vertical line more than once and the six-figure numbers produced in each horizontal, vertical and corner-to-corner line can be divided exactly by 11 when read either forwards or backwards.

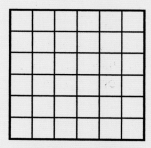

111111   222222
444444   555555
777777   888888

Calculation

If these two numbers total 8679, what do the two numbers below total?

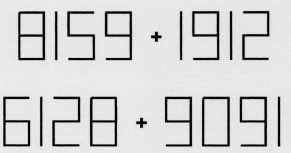

Work It Out

I take what has been projected upwards by a member of the Talpidae family and, in a very short time, create what a major orogeny has taken centuries to produce during the earth's geological history. What am I doing?

Rebuses 2

A rebus is an arrangement of letters or symbols that is used to indicate a word or phrase; for example, bbbbbbbbbb = beeline. What are the following well-known phrases?

1 A (with dot)	**2** M A E L	**3** T E N AN T
4 A TOWN M N	**5** LOOSE LOOSE	**6** MEAS
7 TOCCDUN	**8** F♪	**9** HE AC
10 prEROgative	**11** O E T D R A	**12** NDEX
13 ND PAR	**14** THREE NINE	**15** PART HOME
16 DAUCSTTIROINAL	**17** S E A S S E A (NO) A E S E S A E	**18** BLOUSED
19 RD	**20** ECNALG	**21** TH TH

Lewis

If Lewis is driving a Volkswagen car with the license plate ML8ML8, what model is the car and what color is it?

Letter Sequences 2

1. What two letters complete the sequence NLN, RLN, CTAD?

2. What two letters continue the sequence AUR, ERAY, AC, PI, A, UE?

Number Sequences

1. What number is next in this list? 0,1,8,11,69,88,96,101

2. What number is next in this list? 1,2,5,8,11,22

DIAGRAMS

The type of diagrammatic tests in this section are known as culture-fair tests, and they are widely used in intelligence testing. Their advantage is that they use logic instead of word knowledge, and they are thus more accessible to all members of the community. These tests are considered to be just as reliable as verbal tests, because spatial understanding and logical reasoning are a good guide to levels of intelligence.

If at first you are baffled by these puzzles, stick with them. Even if you cannot work out the answer at the first attempt, it may suddenly click into place if you take a fresh look later.

Analogy 1

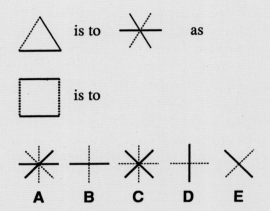

is to   as

is to

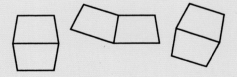

A   B   C   D   E

Logic 3

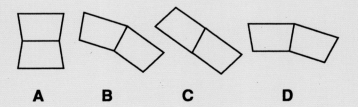

Which figure below continues the above sequence?

A   B   C   D

Missing Square

Find the missing square.

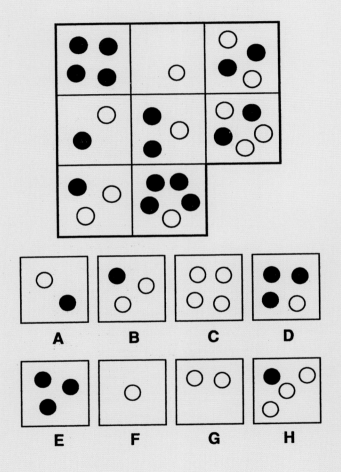

Symbols

Divide each square into four equal portions, each of which will be the same size and shape and will include within it one of each of the five symbols.

1.

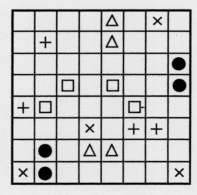

2.

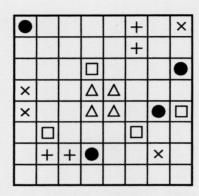

Sequence

Which of the options—A, B, C, D or E—continues this sequence?

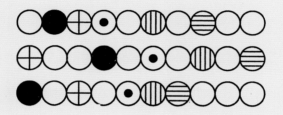

A

B

C

D

E

Dots

What comes next in this sequence, A, B, C, D or E?

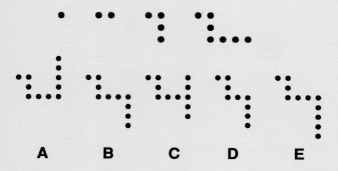

A   **B**   **C**   **D**   **E**

Jigsaw Puzzle

How many different symmetrical figures can be formed by fitting together all the pieces below?

Because pieces can be turned over, you will need to trace and cut out the pieces.

Advance Matrix

Which circle—A, B, C, D, E, F or G—will complete the sequence?

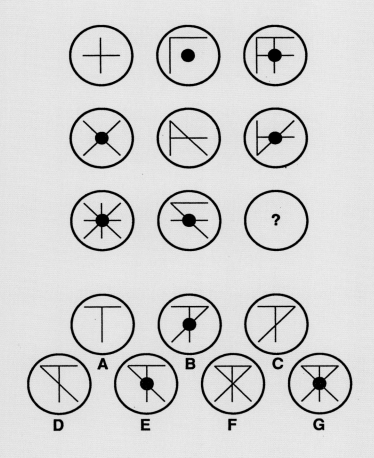

Discs

Which disc—A, B, C, D or E—should come next?

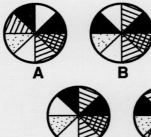

A   **B**   **C**

D   **E**

Peaks

Cut the figure into two identical parts.

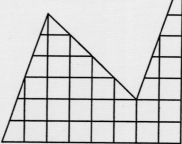

SOMETHING
IN COMMON

In these puzzles all the options given have a strong unifying theme. Again, lateral thinking and flexibility of thought are necessary to enable you to start finding the right answers.

Words

What do the following words have in common with Socrates and Robin Hood?

Quarter
Wednesday
Printer
Nutty
Tuppence
Thirty
Lightning
Quarry

Peoples

What do the people of Belgium have in common with the people of Bangladesh?

Five Words

What do these five words have in common?

Gorge
Funfair
Feminine
Pendent
Besiege

Common Clues 2

What do all the following clues have in common?

1. Foam-crested waves
2. A type of small, very faint, dense star
3. A flag of the Royal Navy
4. A useless possession
5. A high pitch of excitement
6. A termite
7. One who gives financial support in a difficult situation
8. The beluga
9. A pardonable misstatement
10. A government report

Famous Names

What do the following have in common?

Raleigh
Bismarck
Columbus
Lincoln
Montgomery

What's the Link

What do the answers to the following clues have in common?

1. A departure
2. Amounts
3. Arbiters
4. Pity
5. Rulers
6. Records of events
7. Piece of work
8. Traditional sayings
9. A visible impression
10. A disclosing of information

Who's Who

What do the following have in common?

1. A drugged drink
2. Someone who indulges in fantasies
3. A forced selection when there is no alternative
4. A flat, round cake
5. The bottom of the sea
6. A man of high fashion
7. A military officer's wide belt
8. A theater award in the United States
9. A type of petrol bomb
10. A club for elderly people

What's the Connection?

What do a melon, the city of Tokyo and Ronald have in common?

Seven Clues

What links the following clues?

1. Subject to sudden nose spasms
2. Short medic
3. Ill-tempered
4. Content
5. Inclination to slumber
6. Shy
7. Half-asleep

Shortbread and Shooting Stars

What have the following in common?

1. Dresden china
2. Shooting stars
3. Shortbread
4. Jumping bean
5. Lead pencil
6. Bald eagle
7. Horned toads
8. Firefly
9. Prairie dog
10. Catgut

NUMBERS

Numbers can be interesting and challenging. They are often confusing, and they are sometimes manipulated and misrepresented, but at the end of the day mathematics is an exact science, and there is only one correct solution to a correctly set calculation or puzzle.

In this book, we have included a number of magic squares because these are of great interest to us. First developed by the Ancient Chinese, they are arrays of consecutive numbers in which all rows, columns and diagonals add up to the same total. The most famous of these is the order-3 Lo-Shu, which uses the numbers 1-9 once each only to form a 3 x 3 magic square in which each horizontal, vertical and corner-to-corner line totals 15. Do you remember how this square is constructed? (See Numbers Introduction of Mind Bafflers) The Lo-Shu is unique because there is only one possible solution – not counting rotations or reflections, of course, of which there are seven additional versions. As the order of magic squares increases, so do the number of different possible versions—for example, not counting rotations and reflections, there are 880 order-4 squares and over 275 million order-5 squares!

There is a formula for working out the sum of the rows of each magic square. To obtain the constant of a standard order-4 square, add the integers from 1 to 16 and divide the sum by 4—the constant is 34. The constant of an order 5 square is the sum of the numbers 1 to 25 divided by 5—i.e., 65. A further simple formula is that the constant = x (order cubed + order). Therefore, for an order-6 square the constant is (6 x 6 x 6) +6 divided by 2 = 111.

Before you tackle the puzzles that follow, here is one additional gentle warm up magic-square puzzle. The grid below contains the numbers 1 to 16 once each only, but alas only five of the lines add up to 34. Your task is to divide the square into four equal-shaped sections and then to reassemble the four sections to form a true magic square in which each horizontal, vertical and corner-to-corner line totals 34.

13	7	10	4
15	2	12	5
8	9	3	14
1	11	6	16

Magic Square 2

Insert the remaining numbers from 1 to 25 to form a magic square in which each horizontal, vertical and corner-to-corner line totals 65.

				15
10				
	5			
		25		
			20	

The Square Series

What connection do square numbers have with the series 1,4,9,7,7,9,4,1,9?

Athletes

At the athletic meeting, Britain beat Romania by 35 points to 31. Under a new scoring system, Britain took four first places, three second places and one third place. How many events were there, and how were the points for first, second and third places allocated?

Square Numbers 2

Can you find the lowest nine-digit square number that uses the digits 1 to 9 once each only, and then find the highest square number to use the same nine digits?

One Hundred

There are 11 ways of expressing the number 100 as a number and fraction using the nine digits once each only. For example,

$91+ {}^{5823}\!/_{647} = 100$

How many of the other 10 ways can you find? Nine of the ways involve the use of a number above 80 (as shown in the example above, which uses the number 91); one way involves the use of a number less than 10.

Day Finder

On which day of the week did 31 December 1999 fall? Calculate it without looking at a calender.

Connections 2

Insert the numbers 0 to 10 in the circles so that for any particular circle the sum of the numbers in the circles connected directly to it equals the value corresponding to the number in that circle as given in the list below.

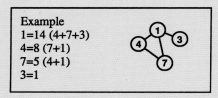

Example
1=14 (4+7+3)
4=8 (7+1)
7=5 (4+1)
3=1

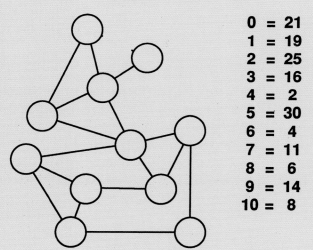

0 = 21
1 = 19
2 = 25
3 = 16
4 = 2
5 = 30
6 = 4
7 = 11
8 = 6
9 = 14
10 = 8

Magic Square 3

Insert the remaining numbers from 1 to 25 to form a magic square in which each horizontal, vertical and corner-to-corner line totals 65.

				15
	5			
		20		
10				
		25		

Missing Number 2

Study the numbers in each horizontal and vertical line and work out the missing number.

15	8	5
4	15	4
4	5	?

ANAGRAMS

Why is AH, SPOTTING HOT NEWS a particularly appropriate phrase? (See Anagrams Introduction of Mind Bafflers 1)

Invented by the Greek poet Lycophron in A.D. 280, anagrams have been popular throughout history. The best ones are those in which the rearranged letters bear some relationship to the original—for example, the word INCOMPREHENSIBLE can be arranged into the phrase PROBLEM IN CHINESE; the phrase I AM A PENCIL DOT is an anagram of A DECIMAL POINT; and WINSTON LEONARD SPENCER CHURCHILL is an anagram of AND—WE'LL COPE 'N' CRUSH HITLER IN SCORN. One of the compilers of this book describes himself as an ESTIMATING ENIGMATIST.

Before you tackle the anagrams that follow, why not try your hand at compiling an anagram yourself? Between 1804 and 1806 a journey of exploration across the American continent was made by Meriwether Lewis and William Clark. Promoted by Thomas Jefferson, the expedition took the explorers over the Rockies, down the Columbia River to the Pacific, explored the Yellowstone River on the return journey, and went on to establish the American claim to the Louisiana Purchase. It was known as THE LEWIS AND CLARK EXPEDITION. Can you use all these 26 letters once each only to make an appropriate phrase? For our solution (4, 6, 5, 7,4) see Anagrams Introduction of Mind Bafflers 2.

Reverse Anagram

If we presented you with the words MAR, AM and FAR and asked you to find the smallest word that contained all the letters from which these words could be produced, we would expect you to come up with the word FARM. Here is a further list of words: CHAIR, CLAY, CARD and CRUSH. What is the smallest word from which all these four words can be produced?

Anagrammed Phrases

Each of the following is an anagram of a well-known phrase, for example:

OIL SHIPS TART = TO SPLIT HAIRS.

1. FASHION BOTTOM CAP
2. SOUR EVERY SIGHT
3. TON IT O GRABBER
4. MILD HIKE GREAT
5. YARK THIRIDMAN DOC.

Words

The following are all one-word anagrams

14-letter words

1. Not a stair I mind
2. Hit blue sex gain
3. Crop sender once
4. Promise I rap Pat
5. Need permit rate

15-letter words

1. Note a crime graph
2. His stroppy cheat
3. Export men in a tie
4. Liven cheery mops
5. I start a main toil

Anagrams

1. VACATE PRO TEM (2 words)

2. CUCKOO TWIRL SCENE (2 words)

3. HE NOTICED HIS COMB WAS ON EDGE (1 word; the anagram is only part of the phrase)

I'll Make a Wise Phrase

Each of the following is an anagram of a play by Shakespeare.

1. Gear link
2. Listen did cross aura
3. Had a mooning butt, ouch!
4. Solvers all boot us
5. Cheery or frets doom

6. Let the rains wet
7. Cool us rain
8. Adjoin me to rule
9. Fathom tension
10. So I cut and it runs

Spherical

Complete the word in each column. All the words end in S, and the scrambled letters in the section to the right of each column can be arranged to form a word that will give you a clue to the word you are trying to find to fit in the column.

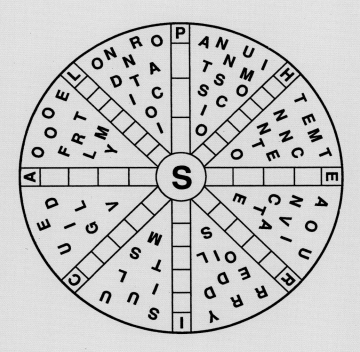

Anagrammed Synonyms

Study the following list of three words. Your task is to find the two out of the three words that can be paired to form an anagram of another word, which is a synonym of the word remaining. For example, in the group LEG – MEEK – NET, the words LEG and NET are an anagram of GENTLE, which is a synonym of the remaining word MEEK.

1. DOTE – GRIT – FRUIT
2. DIVE – MET – LUMP
3. REIN – RIOT – HEART
4. SIP – DIE – HER
5. SOOT – INSIPID – MOOD
6. PAPER – PLAIN – TAN
7. CLIP – LAIR – CUT
8. ROPE – START – PRONE
9. PET – OUR – TEAM
10. CAD – MATE – MORE
11. PLAN – TOP – NICE
12. OLD – TAN – NICE
13. GEMS – SEA – NOTE
14. ATE – URGE – RENT
15. DEED – LONE – REST

Anagram Theme

In each of the following, arrange the 14 words in pairs so that each pair is an anagram of another word or name. The seven words produced will have a linking theme. For example, if the words DIAL and THAN were in the list they could be paired to form an anagram of THAILAND and the theme would be countries.

1.

CHIN	PIT
COOL	RIP
CRIB	RUN
CULT	SAP
HALLS	SNAP
HARD	TEE
IS	TO

2.

ADD	HAS
AGO	LID
APE	RACE
BARN	RIM
BEER	RUG
BUN	STAIN
GLAD	TEN

Anagrammed Quotation

This quotation from William Wordsworth's ode "Intimations of Immortality" has had 10 words removed, all of which have been anagrammed. Can you solve the 10 anagrams below, which are in no particular order and which are all one-word answers, and then restore them to their correct place in the quotation?

Our noisy tears seem _____ in the being
Of the _____ _____ : truths that wake,
To _____ never:
Which _____ _____ , nor mad _____ ,
Nor Man nor Boy,
Nor all that is at _____ with joy,
Can utterly _____ or _____ !

1. Tiny me
2. Tom's men
3. Sob hail
4. Therein
5. Stills senses
6. Len's ice
7. He rips
8. Rent ale
9. Red toys
10. Over a dune

BRAINBENDERS

Every production of genius must be the production of enthusiasm.
—*Benjamin Disraeli*

Genius is one percent inspiration and ninety-nine percent perspiration.
—*Thomas Alva Edison*

To solve the selection of puzzles in this section, which have just one thing in common—their fiendishly high degree of difficulty—you will require enthusiasm, inspiration and a certain amount of perspiration.

A Magic "260"

Insert the remaining numbers from 1 to 64 to form a magic square in which each horizontal, vertical and corner-to-corner line totals 260.

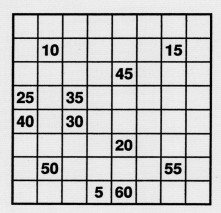

Game Show

You are on a game show and are shown three doors. There is a car behind one door and a goat behind each of the other doors.

You select door number 1, and your chances of finding the car are 2 to 1 against.

The game show host opens door number 2 and reveals a goat. Now your chance of winning the car has reduced to even money.

The host now invites you to change doors to number 3 if you wish. Should you change doors?

Mathematicians

Six mathematicians sat around a table discussing their ages. Those who were over 40 years of age were truthful unless their ages were a multiple of 17; those who were under 40 years of age lied unless their ages were divisible by 13. None of the mathematicians was over 70 years old. The total of their ages was 261. Each mathematician said:

1. Number 5 is older than I am.
2. Number 1 is 30 years younger than Number 3.
3. I am 51.
4. Number 3 is 52. I am not 29.
5. Number 1 is a prevaricator. Number 6 is 39.
6. Number 4 is wrong. Number 2 is 39.

How old were they?

Factorial

What is unusual about the number 5913? Clue: try factorials—i.e., 3! = 3 x 2 x 1.

An Ancient Fraction

For what purpose did the ancient Chinese use the fraction $355/13$, and how is exactly the same result arrived at by using the integers 3, 7 and 16?

Stair-rods

"It's raining stair-rods," said Jim. "If it were," said Sid, "I could use them with this tape measure to calculate the area of that small puddle on the lawn." What method did Sid have in mind for calculating the area of the puddle?

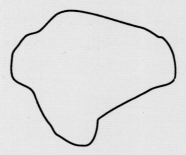

Numbers 2

Four natives on an island were asked to explain their system of numbers.

Native 1 said: "18 is a prime number and so is 41."
Native 2 said: "7 x 8 = 62."
Native 3 said: "35 is a prime number."
Native 4 said: "63 is evenly divisible by 4."

Two of the natives were telling the truth; two of the natives were lying. What is the base of their system?

Analogy

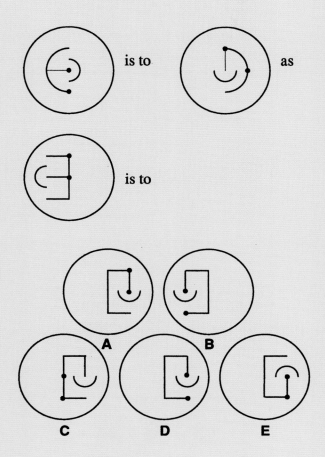

Square of the Sixth Order

Insert the remaining numbers from 1 to 36 to produce a magic square in which each horizontal, vertical and corner-to-corner line totals 111.

	35				
30					
		15			
			20		
		10			25
				5	

Brain Strain 2

Insert numbers into the remaining blank squares so that all the calculations are correct, reading both across and down. All the numbers to be inserted are less than 10.

	−		+		=	4
×		×		+		+
	+		−	3	=	
÷		÷		−		−
	÷	2	+		=	
=		=		=		=
9	−		+		=	

Thirteenth-Century Word Search

Definitions are given for 16 words, all of which date from the thirteenth to the seventeenth century. The words run in any direction in the grid but only in a straight line. Every letter is used, and some are used twice.

1. The person who cries aim at archery
2. A lovely maiden, a pretty lass
3. Food, provisions
4. To sing and weep at the same time
5. To crawl into the skin of another
6. Fingernails
7. Cackles
8. Food and drink that makes one idle (junk food)
9. A tale that evokes joy and sadness
10. Depression of the spirits
11. Freckles, pimples
12. A little darling or mistress
13. A fancy dresser
14. A licentious man
15. Glances of the eye
16 Places for storing ammunition, usually surrounded by high walls

Y	T	N	I	A	D	E	M	K	C	I	R	P
R	F	E	L	L	O	W	F	E	E	L	R	E
R	L	E	U	S	E	L	F	R	U	M	E	R
O	E	N	B	S	P	R	U	W	Y	R	B	U
S	S	O	B					L	E	M	E	
O	H	B	E					L	I	I	L	
G	S	I	R					O	R	T	P	
Y	P	L	W					L	C	Y	T	
R	A	L	O					P	M	L	N	
R	D	E	R	S	P	M	U	T	O	I	L	A
E	E	B	T	S	K	A	E	K	P	A	E	H
M	S	M	E	L	L	S	M	O	C	K	B	C
S	E	L	B	B	U	F	E	L	B	B	U	M

CROSSWORD VARIATIONS

Crossword puzzles are probably the best known type of puzzle in existence, and they are attempted by an enormous number of people every day all over the globe and in all different languages. There are no conventional crosswords in this section, although each puzzle is a variation on the traditional crossword theme.

Nursery Rhyme Crossword 3

Hidden in the narrative are eight clues. Find them, solve them and enter the solutions in the grid.

Jack Sprat, who owned a Greek warship and was one of the excavators, could eat no fat.

His best loved wife, who was one of several young ladies and who was drugged, could eat no lean, and so between them they planned to lick the platter clean of Atlantic fish, from which she extracts essences.

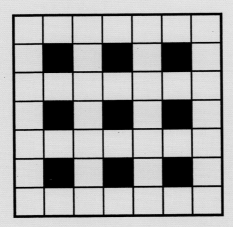

Alphabet Crossword

Insert the 26 letters of the alphabet in the grid to complete the crossword. Seven letters have already been put in place, and one clue is given.

Clue: American drink of spirit and mint.

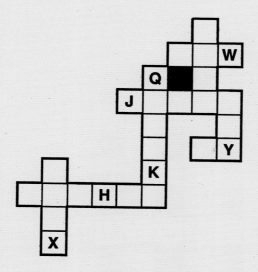

A B C D E F G H̶ I J̶ K̶ L M
N O P Q̶ R S T U V W̶ X̶ Y̶ Z

Diamond Crossword

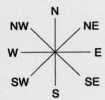

In this unusual crossword all the answers run in the direction of compass points. There are just enough clues to enable all 36 squares to be completed.

Clues:

1. NE Gloomy
1. SE Specimen
3. NE Of time, pass
5. NW Get free
3. N Landed property
1. E Type of light cake
6. W Pal
7. S Region
2. S Dull blow
4. W Rhythmic comnosition

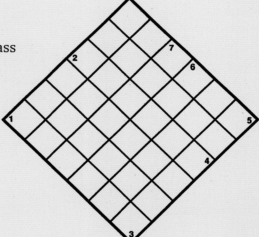

Cross-Alphabet 2

Insert the 26 letters of the alphabet once each only to form a crossword.

Clues (in no particular order):

Invigorating excitement
Expeditiously
Undulating
Bovine mammal
Fear and trembling
Seed case
Stoop
A preserve

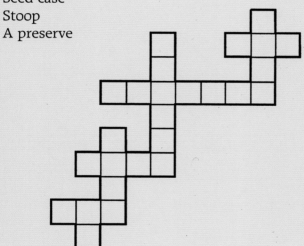

Clueless Crossword 2

In each square are four letters. Your task is to cross out three of the four, leaving one letter in each square so that the crossword is made up of interlocking words in the usual way.

ST RP	IR AE	BQ RS	TA UR	PJ AE	CK RD	AT EN
OR IU	■	EO RU	■	NE MA	■	AJ MC
ET DR	EA WR	OI SA	SM UA	GB PE	AI TL	SE NT
AG NL	■	IS VT	■	OE LF	■	PC NE
LN ET	XN AM	EN TS	ER SA	DY NE	ER AO	ET DN

Target Crossword

Find 16 six-letter words by pairing up the 32 three-letter bits.

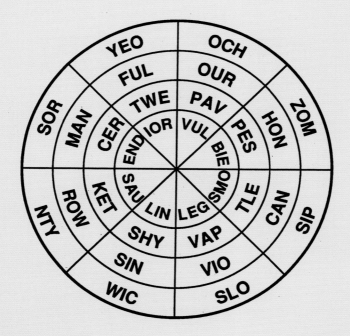

Tiles

Place the tiles in the grid to complete the crossword.

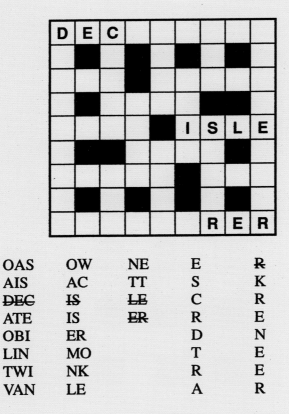

OAS	OW	NE	E	R̶
AIS	AC	TT	S	K
D̶E̶C̶	I̶S̶	L̶E̶	C	R
ATE	IS	E̶R̶	R	E
OBI	ER		D	N
LIN	MO		T	E
TWI	NK		R	E
VAN	LE		A	R

Nursery Rhyme Crossword 4

Hidden in the narrative are eight clues. Find them, solve them and enter the solutions in the grid.

The owl and a certain type of armadillo went to sea in a precious stone color green boat, which was used to lift up mud from the sea bed. They took with them some honey and some tough, white flexible tissue and plenty of small Middle-Eastern coins wrapped up in a five pound note. The armadillo became sorrowful because they could not find the sea-side places.

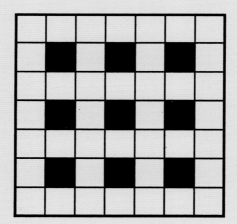

Alphabet Crossword 2

Complete the crossword using all 26 letters of the alphabet once each only, apart from the letters that have already been inserted.

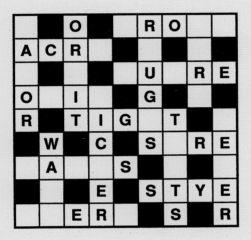

ABCDEFGHIJKLM
NOPQRSTUVWXYZ

Directional Crossword

The answers run horizontally, vertically or diagonally, to either the right or the left. Each solution starts on the lower number and finishes on the next high number—i.e., 1 to 2, 2 to 3, and so on.

1. Keeper
2. Incubus
3. Turned to account
4. Cause anxiety
5. Echinoderm with five arms
6. Female entitled to legacy
7. Firmer
8. Fanatical
9. Disputes
10. Railway carriages storage places
11. Orange-yellow
12. Bird's home
13. Attempted
14. Fish
15. Fixes tightly
16. Flat thick stone
17. Marshy ground

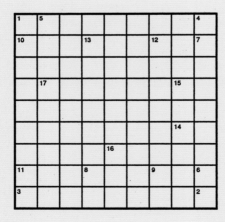

Magic Word Square

Rearrange the 25 letters to form five different five-letter words, which, when placed correctly in the second grid, form a magic word square in which the five words read the same both across and down.

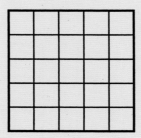

A	V	E	R	T
T	R	I	P	E
S	L	E	E	P
S	P	I	N	E
P	A	V	E	S

Pyramid Quotation

Life is like a tennis game, you can't win without serving.

Use all 45 letters of the above quotation to complete the pyramid with one one-letter, one two-letter, one three-letter, one four-letter, one five-letter, one six-letter, one seven-letter, one eight-letter and one nine-letter word. The clues are in no particular order.

Clues:

Soft and smooth
Artificial hair
Garden flower
Unrestrained and vicious
The pronoun of the first person singular
Sensible
Undecided
Musical composition
Belonging to me

Magic Squares 2

Here are five connected 5 x 5 magic squares. The answers are all five-letter words, and each of the grids reads the same across and down. The clues are given in sets of five, which, in each set, are in no particular order.

Clues 1-5
Diminish
Fence of bushes
Severe or cruel
Cause sharp pain
Swift

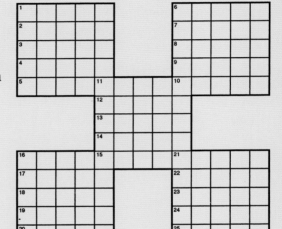

Clues 6-10
Nude
Finished
Religious
Dwelling place
Once more
Sift and strain

Clues 16-20
English royal house
Cosmetic red powder
Warehouse
Made a mistake
Smell

Clues 11-15
Eastern person
Horseman's spear
Huge person
Come into
Bird of prey

Clues 21-25
Love intensely
Regular arrangement
Large forest plants
Oven bake
Work for

WIND-UPS

"Write that down," the King said to the jury, and the jury eagerly wrote down all three dates on their slates, and then added them up, and reduced the answer to shillings and pence.
—Lewis Carroll (Alice's Adventures in Wonderland)

In this final section we present another miscellany of different types of puzzles. We hope that we have not wound you up or muddled you up too much. Rather we hope that we have managed to provide you with some mental relaxation and stimulation and that you have been able to come up with many of the correct solutions.

Our object has been, first and foremost, to provide entertainment. At the same time we hope that you may have learned something along the way and have increased your mental prowess and problem-solving capabilities.

Cryptogram

This appears to be one of those cryptograms in which each letter of the alphabet is substituted by another. Can you solve it?

M ISC HIEV OUSO FM
ETOT RYTOTR ICKY OU

Just for interest, the frequency table for letters of the English language is as follows:

ETAOINSRHLDCUMFPGWYBVKXJQZ

The Eternal Mozart

My compact disc player has a shuffle facility whereby it plays the tracks on a compact disc in random order. Alternatively, if I wish I can program it so that the tracks can be played in any order I want. My favorite Mozart CD has 10 tracks. If I decided to play the disc once each day and program the 10 tracks to be played in a different order each day, how long would it take before I had heard the 10 tracks played in every possible different order?

Cannon Ball

A cannon ball is fired from a cannon and travels for 34 miles horizontally before falling to earth. At the same time as the first cannon ball is fired, a second cannon ball is dropped vertically from the same height as the mouth of the cannon.

Which cannon ball hits the ground first?

The Journey

My pleasant journey commences when I briefly meet a familiar character in front of a wooden strip. I then pass several apartments with many whimsical fancies among a fine array of glossaries. Often feeling a tremble, I find many keen edges between several siestas. My journey ends when I reach a place of refreshment. Where has my journey taken me?

Nine Trees 2

"Take nine conifers from the nursery," said the head gardener to his assistant, **"and plant them so that there are 10 straight rows with three trees in each row."** **"I think that's impossible,"** said the assistant. **"Not at all,"** said the head gardener, **"there is a perfectly symmetric way in which it can be done, but I'll let you work it out for yourself."**

How did the gardener's assistant carry out the task he had been given?

Drinks

Each horizontal line and each vertical line contains the jumbled letters of a type of drink, alcoholic or otherwise. Find the 20 drinks. Every letter in the grid is used once only.

G	U	U	R	U	R	D	R	M	E
I	C	T	M	K	G	L	N	Q	P
E	O	F	C	C	E	Y	C	A	F
A	C	D	C	R	E	I	B	E	J
E	T	T	A	P	A	A	E	U	L
O	O	P	O	T	S	R	Y	H	U
R	M	S	A	N	N	I	A	T	I
L	A	G	I	H	N	H	N	S	I
R	E	O	D	M	U	N	A	S	D
Y	O	S	L	R	H	S	D	E	R

Crazy Columns

Insert the four missing letters in the grid below.

A	G	H	E
I	N	C	O
C	B	P	C
P		O	B
M	L	O	C
	L	P	E
L	D	O	O
T	P	I	E
S		A	E
M	D	H	O
E	O	U	I
S	A		K

Palindromic Years

1991 was a palindromic year, as was the year 2002—a gap of 11 years. When was the last time there was a shorter gap betwen two palindromic years, and when will be the next time?

Frankenstein's Creation

For his latest creation Frankenstein takes a large portion from Trudy, a piece from Hermione, a slice from the middle of Brenda and a small part from Peggy. After he has put them all together, what does Frankenstein call his new creation?

What the Dickens!

By starting somewhere in the letter-maze and by moving one letter at a time to the left or right, or, up or down it is possible to spell out the titles of 10 works by Charles Dickens. It does not matter which title you identify first; provided you make the correct turnings, the titles will eventually lead you through the whole pattern of 144 letters.

B	E	Y	A	N	H	O	S	N	I	C	K
M	O	D	S	D	C	L	A	H	T	Y	L
I	S	T	O	N	I	Z	Z	E	O	B	E
W	T	R	N	T	E	L	U	D	L	I	O
O	L	E	H	I	W	C	H	C	U	R	S
S	I	V	A	R	I	N	H	S	Y	T	I
E	I	T	I	D	T	R	O	P	V	I	D
O	F	O	C	T	I	A	M	D	A	O	C
E	T	W	X	E	M	E	S	N	R	P	P
L	A	T	P	T	A	G	D	A	A	R	E
N	S	A	E	C	E	E	U	B	B	F	I
O	I	T	A	T	R	G	R	Y	D	L	E

Answers

31 Lines
Start at line 31

The 36-Coin Puzzle

2520
2520 is the lowest number into which all the digits from 1 to 10 will divide.

'A' Frame
Across: Banal, Canard, Hazard, Arab, Dastard, Amass, Lascar. Down: Ananas, Abyss, Adamant, Canal, Walls, Jack, Macaw Across answers are ringed. Down answers are not ringed.

Abracadabra
$2^{10} = 1024$

Acrostic
Think   Huff   Oar
Millet   Authority   Shun
Chested   Athos   Ravine
Either   Waggle
Quotation: 'Here lies a king that ruled, as he thought fit, The universal monarchy of wit.'
Author: Thomas Carew

Advance Matrix
C—the outlines in the first column are added to those in the second column. However, lines and the dot disappear where they correspond so that lines and a dot appear in the third column only when they are different.

Advanced Matrix
G.

There are two separate elements in this puzzle. Taking the black and white circles inside the enclosure, there are three different possible combinations, and one each of these combinations appears on each horizontal and vertical line. This is the first element of the puzzle. The second and more complex part is to work out what is happening with the 'X' and '0' symbols outside the enclosure. The last square in each horizontal and vertical line is produced as follows: when two circles or two crosses appear in the same position in the first two parts of each line, a symbol appears in the same position in the third and final part but is changed from a circle to a cross, or vice versa. For example, looking along line one the first and second parts both contain a circle top left. so in the third part a symbol appears in the same position, but is a cross. In the same line a cross appears in the first and second parts top right, so in the third part a symbol appears in the same position, but is a circle. This procedure is repeated in each horizontal and vertical line.

Ages
18

Ale Inn Cans Code
Although it is not a particularly sophisticated code, it was, nevertheless, not deciphered. What is necessary is to start at the end and continue to the beginning, paying attention to the sounds of the words. Note that the word 'flesh' was, in those days, commonly used instead of the word 'meat'. The message read:
Major-General Bumside, Acquia Creek, Va. If I should be in boat off Acquia Creek at dark tomorrow, Wednesday evening, could you without inconvenience, meet [flesh] me and pass an hour or two with me. —A. Lincoln

Alphabet
1. Dock 2. Hope 3. Salary 4. Haze 5. Guitar 6. Jaw 7. Qualm 8. Box 9. Fauna 10. Dove

Alphabet Crossword

Alphabet Crossword 2

Alphametics
1.135) 2970 (22
    270
    270
    270
2.13) 8290 (637
    78
    49
    39
    100
    91
    9

Anagram Theme
1. Radish (is hard); parsnip (rip snap); spinach (chin sap); turnip (pit run); shallot (to halls); broccoli (cool crib); lettuce (tee cult) 2. Dublin (lid bun); Santiago (stain ago); Athens (has ten); Belgrade (glad beer); Canberra (race barn); Prague (rug ape); Madrid (add rim)

Anagram Themes

a. The theme is mammals: Beaver (rave be), Porcupine (upper coin), Whale (he law), Dolphin (hold pin), Anteater (neat rate), Leopard (role pad), Muskrat (rum task)

b. The theme is American presidents: Reagan (age ran), Garfield (gild fear), Harding (rig hand), Madison (maid son), Truman (run mat), Monroe (no more), Washington (showing tan).

Anagrammed Phrases

1. A foot in both camps; 2. Serves you right; 3. To bring to bear; 4. Like grim death; 5. Tom Dick and Harry.

Anagrammed Quotation

The words go into the passage in the following order – moments (2), eternal (8), silence (6), perish (7), neither (4), listlessness (5), endeavor (10), emnity (1), abolish (3), destroy (9).

Anagrammed Synonyms 1

1. Apron – Pinafore 2. Out – Elsewhere 3. Call – Proclaim 4. Send – Transmit 5. Soak – Permeate 6. Sober – Temperate 7. Meek – Gentle 8. Late – Deceased 9. Wit – Badinage 10. Par – Standard 11. Head Cranium 12. Cup – Trophy 13. Smell – Redolence 14. Lark – Escapade

Anagrammed Synonyms 2

1. Grit – fortitude; 2. Dive – plummet; 3. Heart – interior; 4. Die – perish; 5. Mood – disposition; 6. Plain – Apparent; 7. Clip – curtail; 8. Prone – prostrate; 9. Team – troupe; 10. Mate – comrade; 11. Top – pinnacle; 12. Old – ancient; 13. Note – message; 14. Urge – entreat; 15. Lone – deserted

Anagrams

1. Caveat emptor; 2. counter clockwise; 3. ctenoid (an anagram of NOTICED; it means with a comb-shaped edge)

Anagrams Introduction of Intelligence Challengers

Bayonet

Anagrams Introduction of Mind Bafflers 1

The Washington Post

Anagrams Introduction of Mind Bafflers 2

Take Indian child, explore West

Analogy 1

B – the sides of the first figure are parallel with those in the second figure.

Analogy 2

D

An Ancient Fraction

The fraction produces a number that is a fairly accurate approximation of pi – it is within 1.0000000848 of its value. Another way of arriving at the same figure – 3.1415929 – is by using the integers 3, 7 and 16. Take the reciprocal of 16 (i.e., $1 \div 16 = 0.0625$) and add 7=7.0625. Take the reciprocal of this number (i.e., $1 \div 7.0625 = 0.1415929$) and add 3 = 3.1415929.

An Angle on a Cube

At first glance it looks like a 90° right-angle, but it is not. If a third diagonal is drawn (AC), an equilateral triangle is created. The answer is, therefore, 60°.

The Ant on the Elastic Band

10.781355 minutes

Length of elastic (in inches)	No. of minutes	Ant has reached (in inches)
6	1	2
9	2	4.5
12	3	7.333333
15	4	10.41667
18	5	13.7
21	6	17.15
24	7	20.74286
27	8	24.46071
30	9	28.28968
33	10	32.21865
36	10.781355	36

Antigrams

1. Melodramatic.   2. Forty-five.
3. Evangelists.   4. Anarchists.
5. Protectionism.   6. Honestly.
7. Desecration.   8. Diplomacy.
9. Spiro Agnew.   10. Within earshot.

Appropriate Anagrams

1. The eyes   2. Fasten your seat belts
3. Hibernated   4. Switchboard
5. Sahara Desert
6. A merry Christmas and a happy New Year
7. Name for ship   8. Venus de Milo

Arabian Knight

* = asterisk (ass to risk)

Arms

D. To spell out the word SEMAPHORE in semaphore.

Athletes

6 events scored at 6 points for first, 3 for second and 2 for third.

Average Speed

37½ m.p.h.
If the distance to be covered is, say, 60 miles and the car is traveling at 50 mph., the journey will take 1 hour 12 minutes. At 30 mph. the same journey will take 2 hours. This means that it takes 3 hours 12 minutes to cover 120 miles or i hour to cover 37½ miles.

The Average Speed Paradox

24 mph. Most people instantly say 25 mph, but this is not correct, as we can see. Let the distance travelled be 60 miles each way.
Therefore, the journey out = $\frac{90}{20}$ = 3 hours
Therefore, the 120-mile journey = 120, = 24 mph

BC/AD

79 years (there was not a year 0)

Bath

Yes, in 166 seconds
54 seconds = 09 minutes, reciprocal* = 1.11
48 seconds = 08 minutes, reciprocal = 1.25
add 2.36
30 seconds = 05 minutes, reciprocal = 2.00
Reciprocal = 2.777 minutes deduct 0.36
= 166 seconds
* In mathematics, a reciprocal is a number or quantity which, when multiplied by a given number or quantity, gives the product of 1, that is, 08 X 1.25 = 1. To find the reciprocal of 0.8, it is necessary to

divide 1 by 0.8, which gives the reciprocal 1.25.

Beheadments
Wheat, heat, eat

Bezzel's Eight Queens Problem
The number of different solutions is 12 (as shown) and the number of pieces is eight. This is determined by the number of squares along the sides – i.e., a 4 x 4 square would require four pieces.

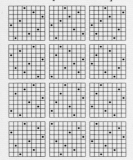

The Bookworm
2$^{1}/_{2}$ inches – i.e., through four covers and one set of pages.

Brain Strain 1

Brain Strain 2

The Broken Clock Face

Each piece totals 20.

The Caesar Alphabet
'All bad precedents began as justifiable measures' (which is attributed to Julius Caesar himself).

Calculation
9825 – turn the page upside down and add up the two numbers.

Calendice
The other numbers on dice 1 are 0, 6, 7 and 8; on dice 2 they are 0, 1 and 2. The 6 serves also as a 9.

Cannon Ball
Both cannon balls hit the ground at the same time.

The Capital and Labor Puzzle
Number the men from 1 to 6, starting at the top. The sequence is then:

1. 1 takes over 2 and returns with the boat.
2. 1 takes over 3 and returns with the boat.
3. 4 and 5 go over, and 4 brings back 2.
4. 4 takes 1 over and brings back 3.
5. 4 and 6 go over, and 1 brings back the boat.
6. 1 takes over 2 and brings back the boat.
7. 1 takes over 3.

Carousel

Including Sammy, there were 13 children on the carousel, as can be seen from the diagram.
$^{1}/_{3}$ x 12=4
$^{3}/_{4}$ x 12=9
4+9=13

Carpenter
He worked on 18 days and did not work on 12 days

Carter Cipher
Total up each group of three numbers and take the corresponding letter of the alphabet. Decoded the message reads: 'The paradox is a cunning beast.'

Catching a Thief
The constable took 30 steps. In the same time the thief would take 48, which, added to his start of 27, would have carried him 75 steps. The distance would be exactly equal to 30 steps of the constable.

Categorize 1
Peace, Physics, Chemistry (Nobel Prizes) Amity, Harmony, Concord (Peace) Douglas, Harrier, Comet (Aeroplanes) Astronomy, Star, Planet (Astronomy)

Categorize 2
European currency (punt, pound, mark); boats (smack, barge, tramp); walk (slog, trek, hike); batter (hammer, beat, thrash)

Ceremonial Sword
He purchased a suitcase 36 in × 24 in and placed the sword in diagonally.

Chess Tournament
The names are all anagrams:
Zena le Vue = Venezuela (the Americas)
Dr A. Glebe = Belgrade (Europe)
Rob E. Lumen = Melbourne (Australasia)
Ann Ziata = Tanzania (Africa)

Cinderella
29
When one lot was taken from a total of 89 the remainder was divisible by three. There are only four possibilities:

	A	B	C	D
Total	89	89	89	89
They took	5	14	23	29
Leaving	84	75	66	60
Red	6	50	44	40
Blue	28	25	22	20
Remaining	6	5	5	5
lots	12	6	6	6
	14	12	12	12
	23	23	14	14
	29	29	29	23

Groups must break into a 2 to 1 ratio. Only D fits:

6 + 14 = 20

5 + 12 + 23 = 40

Circles

Both circles are the same size.

Classic Anagrams

1. Alec Guinness. 2. Astronomical observations.
3. Christianity. 4. The countryside. 5. The desert oasis. 6. Desperation. 7. Disintegration. 8. A domesticated animal. 9. Good steel. 10. The Holy Gospel.
11. In the South Sea Islands. 12. Knights of the Round Table. 13. The landing of the Pilgrims.
14. The liquor habit. 15. Madam Curie. 16. Miguel Cervantes de Saavedra. 17. No trespassing. 18. The professional gambler. 19. Rome was not built in a day. 20. The State of North Carolina.

Classic Kickself Introduction 1

The whip

Classic Kickself Introduction 2

In Shylock's bargain for the flesh was found
No mention of the blood that flowed around:
So when that stick sewed in pieces eight,
The sawdust lost diminished from the weight.

Lewis Carroll

Classic Kickself Introduction 3

It is man, who crawls on all fours as a child, walks on two legs as an adult and walks with the aid of a stick in old age.

Classic Kickself Introduction 4

Polish

Classic Kickself Introduction 5

The sentence spelled out reads: 'There is no possible way.'

The Classic Letter H Puzzle

Clueless Cross Alphabet 1

Across: Quacks, Brightly, Fez
Down: Mops, Wavy, Jinxed

Clueless Cross Alphabet 2

Across: Jamb, Chintzy, Elk, Fops
Down: Waxy, Quivers, Dog

Clueless Crossword 1

C	O	N	C	E	R	T
R		I		V		R
A	V	E	R	A	G	E
M		C		D		A
P	R	E	T	E	X	T

Clueless Crossword 2

T	E	R	R	A	C	E
I		O		M		J
T	R	O	U	B	L	E
L		S		L		C
E	N	T	R	E	A	T

Clueless Magic Squares

a.

S	P	O	R	T	S	T	A	F	F
P	A	P	E	R	T	I	L	E	R
O	P	I	N	E	A	L	A	T	E
R	E	N	E	W	F	E	T	E	S
T	R	E	W	S	F	R	E	S	H

b.

S	H	A	F	T
H	U	L	L	O
A	L	L	A	Y
F	L	A	K	E
T	O	Y	E	D

Coded Message

Take the letter immediately after the first vowel in each word to reveal the message: 'Come up and see me some time.'

Coin

A = $^4/_7$

B = $^2/_7$

C = $^1/_7$

(Because A goes first, he has twice the chance that B has. Because B goes second, he has twice the chance that C has – therefore 4 to 2 to 1.)

Coins

There are 2 men, 5 women and 13 children
men+women+children=20 people
men+women+children=20 coins
(no. of men x 3 coins) = (no. of women x $1^1/_2$ coins)
= (no. of children x $^1/_2$ coin) = (2 x 3) + (5 x $1^1/_2$) + (13 x $^1/_2$) = 20 coins

The Collector's Bequest

3121 coins

$3121 - 1 = 3120 \times ^4/_5 =$

$2496 - 1 = 2495 \times ^4/_5 =$

$1996 - 1 = 1995 \times ^4/_5 =$

$1596 - 1 = 1595 \times ^4/_5 =$

$1276 - 1 = 1275 \times ^4/_5 =$

$1020 \div 5 = 204$ for each daughter

Color Problem

In both cases only two.

Common Clues 1

They were all British Prime Ministers: Heath, Home, Eden, Law, Peel, Grey, North.

Common Clues 2

They all begin with white: white horses; white dwarf; white ensign; white elephant; white heat; white ant; white knight; white whale; white lie; white paper

Conditions

A. The three rectangles produce three triangles.

Confusion at the Rectory

The dachshunds are Alec (owned by Bob) and David (owned by Charlie).

Connections 1

Connections 2

Coup de Grâce

The last fact given means that no one married his son and daughter to the son and daughter of the

same friend. Let us call the five friends by their initials. 'Daughter-in-law of the father of A's son-in-law' means 'A's daughter. 'Son-in-law of the father of C's daughter-in-law' means C's son. Then A's daughter is the sister-in-law of B's son, which can only mean that her brother (A's son) married B's daughter. Similarly, C married his daughter to D's son.
Who is the husband of D's daughter? He cannot be C's or A's son. Let us suppose he is B's son. Then C's daughter's mother-in-law is Mrs D, while A's son's mother-in-law is Mrs B. So D's daughter can't have married B's son. It follows that D's daughter married E's son. D's daughter and B's son have a common mother-in-law: Mrs E.
Eugene's daughter is married to Bernard's son.

Couriers
The speeds of the couriers are $^{250}/_7$ and $^{250}/_9$, so their approach speed was:
$250 \, (^1/_7 + ^1/_9) = 250 \times {}^{16}/_{63}$
and they will meet in $^{63}/_{16} = {}^{315}/_{16}$ days

Crazy Columns
Y, P, G and D – the word hippopotamus can be read downwards, alternating between columns 3 and 1; the word accomplished appears in columns 1 and 3; the word encyclopedia in columns 4 and 2; and gobbledegook in columns 2 and 4.

Cricket
444. There are no four-digit palindromic prime numbers, and there are only 15 three-digit palindromic prime numbers and one two-digit palindromic prime number. They are: 11 and 101, 131, 151, 181, 191, 353, 373, 383, 727, 757, 787, 797, 919 and 929. These total 7104, which gives an average of 444.

The Crimean Conundrum
A watch

Cross Alphabet 1
Across: Backs, Jog, Dim, Zephyr Down: Quantify, Slow, Vex

Cross-Alphabet 2

Cross-Numbers

Cryptic Elimination 1
A. Trappist monk B. Principal boy C. Drill sergeant D. Jury-rigged E. Basking shark F. Spoonbill G. Stonewall H. Freelance I. Roadrunner J. Snapdragon K. Red Admiral L. Filing cabinet
Odd word: Squash

Cryptic Elimination 2
A. Snow goose B. Sidestep C. Harebell D. Jaywalking E. Killer whale F. Plimsoll line G. Deerstalker H. Toffee-nosed I. Tightfisted J. Rubber stamp K. Shorthand L. Space woman Odd word: Silver

Cryptogram
Mischievous of me to try to trick you (sorry!)

Cryptograms
1. 'An optimist is a man who starts a crossword puzzle with a fountain pen.'
2. The man who smiles when things go wrong has thought of someone he can blame it on.' *Jones' Law*
3. 'In general, the art of government consists in taking as much money as possible from one party of the citizens to give to the other.' *Voltaire*

Cryptokey 1
'Time flies; I can't, they come past at such irregular intervals' Keyed phrase: Tempus Fugit (TEMPUSFGI)

Cryptokey 2
These two great organisations of the English speaking democracies, the British Empire and the United States, will have to be somewhat mixed up together in some of their affairs... I do not view the process with any misgivings. I could not stop it if I wished; no one can stop it. Like the Mississippi, it just keeps rolling along. Let it roll. Let it roll on in full flood, inexorable, irresistible, benignant, to broader lands and better days.' *Winston Churchill*
Keyed phrase: Hands across the sea (HANDSCROTE)

Cryptosymbol 1
This is a straight substitution cryptogram where each letter of the alphabet is represented by its own symbol. Decoded the quotation reads: 'The least thing upset him on the links. He missed short putts because of the uproar of butterflies in the adjoining meadow.' *P. G. Wodehouse*

Cryptosymbol 2
This is a straight substitution cryptogram in which each letter of the alphabet is represented by a different symbol. Decoded, the quotation reads: 'Mr. Harris, plutocrat wants to give my cheek a pat, if the Harris pat means a Paris Hat, hooray!' *Cole Porter*

Cubes
$73 - 63 - 33 = 100$
$18703 - 17973 - 9033 = 100$

Curiosity in Words

KAI SER	SER BIA
IOF FRE	FRE NCH

Day Finder
This is a simple mathematical problem. There are five variables, each of which affects the day of the week upon which any date falls, and by substituting numbers for those variables we can find the day of the week for any date over a period of 200 years.
Century – an adjustment is needed at each change of century: 1900+ is fixed at 0. 2000+ will require an adjustment of -1 This adjustment covers the first two digits of the year.
Year – we now need to look at the last two digits of the year. Because there are 365 days in the year, which when divided by 7 leaves a remainder of 1.

the same date each year will be advanced by one day – for example January 5, 1922 was a Thursday, January 5, 1923 was a Friday – we therefore take the last two figures as actual – i.e., 99.

Leap year – this occurs every four years, and the jump is therefore two days instead of one day for each year that passes. This is covered by adding $\frac{1}{4}$ of the last two digits of the year and ignoring any remainder – i.e., 99 x $\frac{1}{4}$ = 24.

Day – use the actual day – i.e., 31.

Month – a code is shown for the month as follows, Jan=1, Jan LP=0, Feb=4, Feb LP=3, Mar=4, Apr=0, May=2, Jun=5, Jul=0, Aug=3, Sep=6, Oct=1, Nov=4, Dec=6. Because the effect of a leap year is not felt until February 29, a different code number is used for January and February during leap years. Our calculation is therefore as follows for 31 December 1999.

Century 19=0
Last two digits of year=99
Leap years @ $\frac{1}{4}$=24
Day =31
Month Dec =6
Total =160, divided by 7 gives a remainder of 6
Key: Sun=1, Mon=2, Tue=3, Wed=4, Thur=5, Fri=6, Sat=0
Answer FRIDAY

Diamond Crossword

Dice

14.7 times (the sum of $1 + \frac{6}{5} + \frac{6}{4} + \frac{6}{3} + \frac{6}{2} + \frac{6}{1}$)

The Diophantine Squares

41, 80, 320

Directional Crossword

1. Custodian, 2. Nightmare, 3. Exploited, 4. Distress, 5. Starfish, 6. Heiress, 7. Stiffer, 8. Rabid, 9. Differs, 10. Sidings, 11. Saffron, 12. Nest, 13. Tried, 14. Dab, 15. Beds, 16. Slab, 17. Bog

Discs

B – each section moves in its own individual sequence. The dots move three places anticlockwise; the solid sections move two places clockwise; the cross-hatched sections move one place clockwise; the lined sections move three places anticlockwise; and the white sections move two places clockwise, then two places anticlockwise.

Dishes

60 guests.
$^{(65 \times 12)}/_{13}$= 60
or $\frac{x}{2} + \frac{x}{3} + \frac{x}{4} = 65$ ($\frac{60}{2} + \frac{60}{3} + \frac{60}{4} = 30 + 20 + 15$)

DIY Crosswords

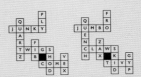

Dodecahedra

Paint Possible ways
Red Blue Faces of painting
12 0 2
11 1 2
10 2 6
9 3 10
8 4 24
7 5 28
6 6 24
96

Dodgson's Podgson's Pillow Problem No. 31

When the clock says 12 hours 2 minutes and 29 $^{277}/_{288}$ secs.

On July 1 my watch gained on the clock 5 minutes in 10 hours i.e., $\frac{1}{2}$ min. per hour or 2 minutes in 4 hours. Hence, when my watch said noon, the clock said 12, hours 2 minutes – i.e., the clock was 3 minutes slow of true time, when the true time was 12 hours 5 minutes. On July 30 the watch lost on the clock 1 minute in 10 hours – i.e., 6 seconds per hour or 19 seconds in 3 hours 10 minutes. Hence, when the watch said 12 hours 10 minutes, the clock said 12 hours 7 minutes 19 seconds – i.e., the clock was 2 minutes 19 seconds fast of true time, when true time was 12 hours 5 minutes. Hence, the clock gains, on true time, 5 minutes 19 seconds in 29 days – i.e., 319 seconds in 29 days – i.e., 11 seconds per day: i.e., $^{11}/_{24}$ x 12 seconds in 5 minutes Hence, while true time goes 5 minutes the watch goes 5 minutes and $^{11}/_{288}$ seconds.

Now, when true time is 12 hours 5 minutes on 31 July, the clock is (2 minutes 19 seconds + 11 seconds) fast of it – i.e., says 12 hours 7 $\frac{1}{2}$ minutes. Hence, if true time be put 5 minutes back, the clock must be put 5 minutes $^{11}/_{288}$ seconds back – i.e., must be put back to 12 hours 2 minutes 29 $^{277}/_{288}$ seconds. Hence, on 31 July when clock indicates this time, it is true noon.

Dots

E – the number of dots increases by one each time, and the dots are added horizontally, vertically downwards, horizontally and, finally, vertically downwards.

Double Acrostic

M inut E
E xclamatio N
N avigat E
T ea R
A spirin G
L ibert Y

Double-Cross Alphabet

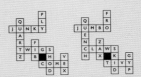

Doublets

1. Nose-note-cote-core-corn-coin-chin. 2. Comb-come-home-hole-hale-hall-hail-hair. 3. Four-foul-fool-foot-fort-fore-fire-five. 4. Lion-limn-limb-lamb. 5. Pity-pits-pins-fins-find-fond-food-good. 6. Many-mane-wane-wale-wile-will-wall-wail-fail. 7. Black-blankblink-clink-chink-chine-whine-white. 8. Flour-floor-flood-blood-brood-broad-bread. 9. River-rover-cover-coves-cores-corns-coins-chins-shins-shine-shone-shore. 10. Kettle-settle-settee-setter-better-betted-belted-bolted-bolter-bolder-holder. 11. Grass-crass-cress-tress-trees-frees-freed-greed-green. 12. Kaiser-raiser-raised-railed-failed-foiled-coiled-cooled-cooked-corked-corker-porker.

Drinks

The letters in across words are circled.

G	U	U	R	U	R	D	R	M	E	RUM
I	C	T	M	K	G	L	N	Q	P	MILK
E	O	F	C	C	E	Y	C	A	F	COFFEE
A	C	D	C	R	E	I	B	E	J	CIDER
E	T	T	A	P	A	A	B	U	L	TEA
Q	O	P	O	T	S	R	Y	H	U	PORT
R	M	S	A	N	N	I	A	T	I	MARTINI
L	A	G	I	H	N	H	N	S	I	GIN
R	E	O	D	M	U	N	A	S	D	MEAD
Y	O	S	L	R	H	S	D	E	R	SHERRY

LAGER COCOA STOUT CORDIAL PUNCH NEGUS SHANDY SQUASH JULEP

Early Arrival

24 minutes.
There are two simple formulas for working out the answer to this puzzle.
(a) Total time difference, 30 minutes, less time saved, 12 minutes – that 5, 18 minutes – plus one halftime saved – that is, 6 minutes = 24 minutes.
(b) Subtract one half time saved, 6 minutes, from total time difference, 30 minutes = 24 minutes.
If you do not know either of the formulas, the answer can be worked out by logic. As I leave according to my usual schedule, we know it is before 5.30 p.m. when I pick up my wife. Because we have saved 12 minutes, that must be the same time that it takes me to drive from the point I picked her up, to the station, and back to that same point. Assuming it takes an equal 6 minutes each way I have therefore picked up my wife 6 minutes before I would normally do so, which means 5.24 p.m. So my wife must have walked from 5 p.m. to 5.24 p.m. or for 24 minutes.

Eight-Pointed Star

The Elusive Lift

It was visiting the floors in the sequence of pi (3.141592).

The Energetic Dog

Like so many puzzles of its type this looks much more complicated than it really is. In fact, it has a beautifully simple solution. The trick is first to work out how long it takes the man to walk home. You know that the dog has been running for all this time at its given constant speed, so it is then a simple matter to work out how many miles it has covered during this period. In this case the man walks for 7 miles at 3 m.p.h., which means he takes $2\frac{1}{3}$ hours or 2 hours 20 minutes. The dog is therefore running for $2\frac{1}{3}$ hours at 8 m.p.h., which means it covers $18\frac{2}{3}$ miles.

The Engine Driver

The passenger who lives nearest the guard is not Petrov (4,5). He does not live in Moscow or Leningrad, since, at best, these are only tied for being nearest to the guard (2). So he is not Ivanov (1). By elimination he is Sidorov. Since the passenger from Leningrad is not Ivanov (1), by elimination he is Petrov. The guard's name is Petrov (3). Since Sidorov is not the fireman (6), by elimination he is the engine driver.

Enigmagram

Pomfret, Herring, Lamprey, Halibut Key anagram: Grouper

Enigmasig 1

Negligence (Carelessness)   Archetype (Prototype)
Ignoble (Dishonorable)   Sample (Specimen)
Gratitude (Thankfulness)   Ignore (Disregard)
Macabre (Gruesome)   Genuine (Authentic)

Enigmasig 2

Noble (Illustrious)   Avarice (Covetousness)
Income (Revenue)   Severe (Rigorous)
Guile (Cunning)   Immobile (Motionless)
Manacle (Handcuff)   Giraffe (Camelopard)

Envelopes

1854. The general formula is: $n!(\frac{1}{2}! - \frac{1}{3}! + \frac{1}{4}! - \frac{1}{5}! + -1^{n}!)$. When n = 7, the value is 1854.

Equation

$7^2=49$ – the 6 has been turned over to turn it into a 9.

The Eternal Mozart

10x9x8x7x6x5x4x3x2x1=3628800 days or 9941 years (excluding leap years)

Excelsior

24 miles; 06:30
A level mile takes $\frac{1}{4}$ of an hour, up hill takes $\frac{1}{3}$ of an hour, down hill takes $\frac{1}{6}$ of an hour. Hence, to go and return over the same mile, whether on the level or on the hill side, takes $\frac{1}{2}$ an hour. Therefore, in 6 hours they went 12 miles out and 12 miles back. If the 12 miles out had been nearly all level, they would have taken a little over 3 hours; if nearly all up hill, a little under 4 hours. Hence 3 hours must be within $\frac{1}{2}$ an hour of the time taken in reaching the peak; thus, as they started at 3, they got there within $\frac{1}{2}$ an hour of 06:30.

Factorial

5913 = 1! + 2! + 3! + 4! + 5! + 6! + 7!

The Famous Farmer's Horses Puzzle

One-half, one-quarter and one-fifth do not add up to unity – i.e., 0.5 + 0.25 + 0.2 = 0.95.

Famous Names

They are all capital cities of states of the United States.

Figure It Out

All begin with the number one in a different language:
(En)umerate – Danish
(Uno)ccupied – Italian and Spanish
(One)rous – English
(Un)usual – French
(Bir)d – Turkish

Filling a Bath

3 minutes. This is solved by reciprocals in the form $(6^{-1} + 4^{-1} - 12^{-1})$-I which is:
$\frac{1}{6} + \frac{1}{4} - \frac{1}{12} = 0.166 + 0.25 - 0.083 = 0.333$
$\frac{1}{0.333} = 3$ minutes

Find Another Word

Bed. All words can be prefixed with Hot.

Find the Lady
Deidre – all the other names appear in US States: Indiana, Maryland and Carolina.

Find the Number
Two thousand nine hundred and forty – MMCMXL

Five 5 x 5 Magic Squares
a.

23	6	19	2	15
4	12	25	8	16
10	18	1	14	22
11	24	7	20	3
17	5	13	21	9

23	6	19	2	15
4	12	25	8	16
10	18	1	14	22
11	24	7	20	13
17	5	13	21	9

b.

R	U	D	E	R	S	O	L	I	D
U	V	U	L	A	O	P	E	R	A
D	U	C	A	T	L	E	G	A	L
E	L	A	T	E	I	R	A	T	E
R	A	T	E	D	D	A	L	E	S

c.

25	10	3	6	21
22	12	19	8	4
11	9	13	17	15
2	18	7	14	24
5	16	23	20	1

d.

14	3	11	13	24
19	23	7	10	6
20	15	1	17	12
4	22	25	9	5
8	2	21	16	18

e.

15	4	20	16	10
2	19	18	23	3
21	25	1	7	11
5	9	14	13	24
22	8	12	6	17

Five Words
They begin with the word five in different languages – Go (Japanese), Fünf (German), Fern (Danish), Pende (Greek) and Bes (Turkish)

Food for Thought
Get out your conversion tables. Convert:

Miles to Centimetres	Tons to Pounds
Acres to Hectares	MALT = CHOP
Litres to Ounces	

Four Teasers
1. 81b
2. Because if number nine had been working the chief engineer would have said 'seven out of eight are not working'.
3. 157–1728 ends give 144 cigarettes; 144 ends give 12 cigarettes; 12 ends give one further cigarette – giving a total of 157.
4. Z–D+3=H+4=M+5=S+6=Z

Fours

1.Cast 2. Song 3. Rest 4. Foot 5. Over 6. Word 7. Hill 8. Wind 9. Rush 10. Face

Fractions
a. $^{3187}/_{25496}$ b. $^{2394}/_{16758}$ c. $^{2943}/_{17658}$ d. $^{6729}/_{13458}$

Frankenstein's Creation
Ermentrude – Hermoine, Brenda, Trudy, Peggy

Game Show
This puzzle was featured in the Mail on Sunday, but was not fully investigated. Half the mathematicians who were consulted favored changing, half did not. This is because there are two possible answers. If the host did not know what was behind each door, then there would be no merit in changing. If, however, the host did know what was behind each door, you should change because your chances double.

The Get Off the Earth Puzzle
As they cross the circumference of the circle, the warriors spiral towards its center. Each man sends forward a larger section of some part of him than he receives, and thus produces an accumulated figure at the end of the line – i.e., the 13 warriors merge into 12 slightly larger warriors.

The Golf Club Statistician
To solve this puzzle it is essential to pick up the opening clue that there were only two preliminary rounds. Therefore, the number of entries for one of the competitions must have been 4, 8, 16, 32, 64 and so on, so that no preliminary rounds were necessary. From there, by some trial and error, it is possible to arrive at the following solution, which is the only one that meets the requirements of the remainder of the puzzle.

Entries	Cube	Players in 1st round	Players in preliminary round	Preliminary round losers	Matches rounds	My rounds
22	10648	10	12	6	21	5
32	32768	32	—	—	31	5
42	74088	22	20	10	41	6
		13				

Consolation event						
16		16	—		$\frac{15}{108}$	16

My handicap = 8; my wife's handicap = 16; club statistician's handicap = 13; Seth Arkwright's age = 108.

Groups
In the cove near hove rafters tend to rake and span and slot home on buildings.
In the same cove your outer charm will be the downfall of a gang of husky gamblers.
You can hear the snide remarks of a wisp of blushing kennel maids as they drift and clamour and mingle and hover and cry at the observance of a dray full of troops.

Coven of Witches	Gam of Whales
Hover of Crows	Earth of Foxes
Rafter of Turkeys	Nide of Pheasant
Erst of Bees	Wisp of Snipe
Rake of Colts	Blush of Boys

Span of Mules
Sloth of Bears
Building of Rooks
Covey of Partridge
Rout of Wolves
Charm of Finches
Down of Sheep
Fall of Woodcock
Gang of Elk
Husk of Hares

Kennel of Raches
Drift of Wild Pigs
Clamour of Rooks
Glean of Herrings
Hover of Crows
Cry of Hounds
Observance of Hermits
Rayful of Knaves
Troop of Foxes

Handshakes
190 (19 + 18 + 17 + 16 + 15 +14 +13 +12 +11 + 10 + 9 + 8 + 7 + 6 + 5 + 4 + 3 + 2 + 1)

Harem
It is not. Consider all the mothers who have only one child. Half of the children will be boys, half girls. Mothers of the girls will then have a second child. Again there will be an even distribution of boys and girls. Half of these mothers will then go on to have a third child and again there will be as many boys as girls. Regardless of the number of rounds and the size of the families, the sex ratio will obviously always be one to one.

Helpuselph
The two adjacent sides of the rectangle total 23 miles. Hence, if 'm' miles be one side of the rectangle (m+4 X 23 -m+ 5) = 2m(23 -m), so 'm' is either 14 or 8. The Governor had in mind a rectangle 15 miles by 8 miles (which is half the area of a rectangle 20 miles by 12 miles). The applicant selected a rectangle 14 miles by 9 miles (which is half the area of a rectangle 18 miles by 14 miles). So the area in question was 126 square miles.

Hexagon

Hexwords

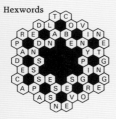

The Hidden Message
Take the fifth word, then count six and take the next word, then count seven and take the next word and so on to reveal the message 'The supplies will arrive early Tuesday morning'.

Hooves

Horse Racing
20-1

Odds Any horse	Odds + stake	Divide each one into loo	Staked amount to win
2½ 100	3½		= 28.57
3½ 100	4½		= 22.22
4½ too	5½		= 18.18
100	6		= 16.67
JO 100	II		= 9.09
16 100	17		= 5.88
20 100	21		= 4.76
20 100	21		= 4.76
100			110.13

(A bookmaker tries to balance his book – that is, by giving odds lower than true odds and taking money on the horses that he wishes to. He can therefore win, whichever horse wins the race. To assess the position at any given time, he finds out how much he would have to take in order to pay $100 on the winner. If the takings are over $100 he will win; if they are under $100 he will lose.)

Houses
7 + 49 + 343 + 2401 + 16807 = 19607

How Old is Mary?
Mary is 27½ years old.

How to Make a Chinese Cross
Place Nos. 1 and 2 close together, as in Fig. 1; then hold them together with the finger and thumb of the left hand horizontally and with the square hole to the right. Push No.3 – placed in the same position "facing you" (a) in No.4 – through the opening at K, and slide it to the left at A, so that the profile of the pieces should be as in Fig. 2.

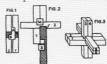

Now push No.4 *partially* through the space from below upwards, as seen in Fig. 2. Place No.5 cross ways upon the part Y, so that the point 2 is directed upwards to the right hand side; then push No.4 quite through, and it will be in the position shown by the dotted lines in Fig. 2. All that now remains is to push No.6 – which is the key – through the opening M and the cross is completed as in Fig. 3.

Hyakugo-Gen

Multiply the first remainder by 70 (2 x 70= 140).
Multiply the second remainder by 21 (1 x 21 = 21).
Multiply the third remainder by 15 (6 x 15=90).
Add the three results (140 + 21 + 90 = 251).
Subtract 105 or its multiple from the sum, in this case its multiple (251-210 = 41 years old).
Incidentally, Hyakugo-Gen in Japanese means 'subtract 105'.

The Hyperion Diamond

I'll Make a Wise Phrase

1. King Lear, 2. Troilus and Cressida, 3. Much Ado About Nothing, 4. Loves Labours Lost, 5. The Comedy of Errors, 6. The Winter's Tale, 7. Coriolanus, 8. Romeo and Juliet, 9. Timon of Athens, 10. Titus Andronicus

The Incredible Square!

It is still a magic square upside down and backwards.

The Jealous Husbands

Let the men be A, B, and C and let the wives be a, b and c.

Bank	Boat	Opposite bank
ACac	Bb	None
ACac	B	b
ABC	ac	b
ABC	a	bc
Aa	BC	bc
Aa	Bb	cc
ab	AB	Cc
ab	c	ABC
b	ac	ABC
b	B	ACac
None	Bb	ACac

Jig Word

Jigsaw Puzzle

3-square, rectangle and Greek cross

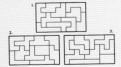

The Journey

Through a piece of music – character = clef; wooden strips = stave; several apartments = flats; whimsical fancies = crochets; array of glossary = notes; tremble = quaver; keen edges = sharps; siestas = rests; public house = bar

Joyville

Denote the girls by their initials and the judges by abbreviations. The following are the possible distributions of 10 votes among 6 competitors with not more than one 0:

a	6	1	1	1	1	0
b	5	2	1	1	1	0
c	5	1	1	1	1	1
d	4	3	1	1	1	0
e	4	2	2	1	1	0
f	4	2	1	1	1	1
g	3	3	2	1	1	0
h	3	3	1	1	1	1
j	3	2	2	2	1	0
k	3	2	2	1	1	1
m	2	2	2	2	2	0
n	2	2	2	2	1	1

Eight thought A the winner. This shows that distributions, a, b, c, d, e, f, j and k must have been used, giving a 34 point for eight judges. It is now clear that Ham's distribution must be h. The remaining distribution must therefore be g, as A's total is four times that of F. We can now see that the totals are: A 40, H 14, M 13, P 12, S 11, F 10.
Now it is clear that Eve's distribution is a, Bas's c, Lio's b and Vic's g, and it therefore follows that Geo's is d or f. F received 3 votes from Ham and 2 from Jim (either e or k), and she received 0 in three cases. As there are only six 0-votes altogether, the three given to F must have been given her by Vic, Eve and Lio; hence Geo's distribution is not d and must therefore be f. She therefore received 1 from each of the others. As Alec gave 0 to S and 1 to F, it is clear that his distribution must have been e (see P's remarks). Thus Jim's must be k.
Now we are left with d and j for Ste and Ted. In either case P must get 3 votes (1 and 2, or 2 and 1) from them; 3 from d would give her too great a total. Hence P receives 1 each from Vic and Lio to make her total right.
We now know that S must receive 3 votes from Vic and Ted, and as only 1 or 3 is available from Vic, since his 2 has gone to M, S receives 1 from Vic and 2 from Ted. Thus Ted's distribution must be j. To get P's total she must receive 1 from Ste, and to get M's total she must receive 3 from Ste and 2 from Lio. The table of distribution is accordingly as follows:

Distribution	c	h	g	k	e	d	j	a	b	f	Totals
JUDGE	Bas	Ham	Vic	Jim	Alec	Ste	Ted	Eve	Lio	Geo	
Annette	5	3	3	3	4	4	3	3	5	4	40
Helen	1	1	3	1	1	1	2	1	2	1	14
Mayblossom	1	1	2	1	2	3	0	1	1	1	13
Prudence	1	1	1	1	2	1	1	1	1	1	12
Sonia	1	1	1	2	0	0	2	1	1	2	11
Fern	1	3	0	2	1	1	1	1	0	0	10

Jumble
Alternative, anticyclone, approximate, allegorical, archaically, arraignment, approbation, acupuncture

Jumping Coins
1. 12 onto 3
2. 7 onto 4
3. 10 onto 6
4. 8 onto 1
5. 11 onto 2
6. 9 onto 5

Keywords
1. Mistaken; 2. Cabbage; 3. Important

Kickself Introduction of Intelligence Challengers 1
The whip

Kickself Introduction of Intelligence Challengers 2
They cannot fall down the hole.

Kickself Introduction of Intelligence Challengers 3
The coin could not have been marked BC before the birth of Christ.

Kickself Introduction of Intelligence Challengers 4
1989 X 50p = £994.50; 1988 x 50p = £994.00

Kickself Introduction of Intelligence Challengers 5
They were triplets, and the third one was a girl.

Kickself Introduction of Intelligence Challengers 6
No doors are shown, so they must be on the opposite side. This would then be the curb side. In Britain the bus would therefore be traveling towards 'B'.

Kickself Introduction of Mind Bafflers
Lewis Carroll made sure that the number he wrote added to the number above it totalled 9999. The answer was therefore bound to be
3144 + 99999999 = 23142

King
Assume that the servant is not included in the count. He arrives at the first manor with no men, so he would collect no men, and the final total would be no men. Therefore, the servant must include himself as the first soldier, and the numbers on leaving each manor increase in the progression 2, 4, 8 and so on. On leaving the thirtieth manor the total would be 2^{30} = 1073741824.

King Jovial's Party
Beginning with King Jovial, the diners were seated clockwise as follows: King Jovial, the Duchess of Dull Ness, the Marquis of Muttonfat, Mrs Toady, Lord Parsley, Queen Cilly, Lord Peekaboo, the Marchioness of Muttonfat, the Duke of Dull Ness, Lady Parsley, Toady and Lady Peekaboo.

The Knight's Dance
A total of 16 moves is necessary:

Knight's Move
The first capture can be of any pawn except C4, D3, D4, E5, E6 or F5. For example, place the knight on A3 and capture C2, B4, D3, B2, C4, D2, B3, D4, E6, G7, F5, E7, G6, E5, F7 and G5 in turn.

The Knight's Tour
More people are coming to, realize how much fun there can be in the solving of simple little math teasers.

Knight's Turn
'The last thing one discovers in writing a book is what to put first.' *Blaise Pascal*

8H-6G-4H-2G-1E-2C-1A-3B-5A-7B-8D-7F

T H E L A S T T H I N G
6H-4G-2H-1F-2D-1B-3A-5B-7A-8C-7E-8G

O N E D I S C O V E R S
6F-7H-8F-7D-8B-6A-4B-2A-1C-2E-1G-3H

I N W R I T I N G A B O
5G-6E-7C-5D-6B-4A-3C-1D-3E-5F-3G-4E

O K I S W H A T T O P U
6D-4C-SE-3F-4D-6C

T F I R S T

23	6	19	2	15
4	12	25	8	16
10	18	1	14	22
11	24	7	20	,3
17	5	13	21	9

The Laborer's Puzzle
At present the hole is 3ft 6in deep and the man is 2ft 4in above ground. When it is complete, the hole will be 10ft 6in deep and the man will be 4ft 8in below the surface.

Labyrinth
a. Notwithstanding
b. Lackadaisically

Lathe
$$\frac{v}{v - 1690} = 14$$

The old time is fourteen times the new, so the new velocity is fourteen times the old.
Therefore v = 1820 inches per minute.

Law of the Search
The Law of the Search: 'The first place to look for anything is the last place you would expect it to be.'

Letter Change
1. Just the job; 2. Fun and games; 3. In full cry; 4. Go like a dream; 5. Run rings around; 6. Tooth and nail; 7. Blow hot and cold; 8. Play on words; 9. Hide and seek; 10. Play with fire; 11. Take in good part;

12. Turn a deaf ear; 13. Name the day; 14. Old wives tale; 15. With open arms; 16. In the raw; 17. Out of order; 18. Live and let live; 19. Get a move on; 20. Any old how

Letter Conundrums
1. T is in the middle of water. 2. L makes a pear into a pearl. 3. S makes our cream sour cream. 4. F comes at the end of beef. 5. C forms lasses into classes. 6. P is the first in pity and the last in help. 7. M. 8. W makes ill will. 9. X is inexplicable. 10. Q goes ahead of U (you). 11. N is at the end of venison. 12. 0. 13. E is at the end of life. 14. B makes it broad. 15. V is invisible. 16. I. 17. Y changes lad to lady. 18. A is in the middle of day. 19. K is at the end of pork. 20. G is in the center of light. 21. D because we could not be wed without it. 22. H because it is in the middle of washing. 23. U is in the middle of fun. 24. Z is the leading feature of the zoo. 25. R is in the middle of labyrinth. 26. J is the first of January.

Letter Sequences 1
1. F – they are the first letters of the words first, second, third, fourth and fifth.
2. A – the letters are extracted from the days of the week in the following sequence: S is the first letter of the first day (Sunday), O is the second letter of the second day (Monday) and so on. A is the seventh letter of the seventh day (Saturday).
3. Z – they are initial letters of the Greek alphabet – alpha, beta, gamma, delta, epsilon and zeta
4. F – they are the first letter of the second names of US presidents in reverse order – Clinton, Bush, Reagan, Reagan, Carter, Ford.
5. J – they are initials of the months arranged first according to the number of days, then in alphabetical order when the number of days is equal. The next month in the list is therefore July.

Letter Sequences 2
1. AE – these are the alternate letters from England, Ireland, Scotland and Wales. 2. UY – these are the alternate letters from the months of the year.

Letters

If each letter is allocated its appropriate number in the alphabet – i.e., A=1, B=2 and so on – a magic square is formed whereby each horizontal, vertical and corner-to-corner line totals 34.

Letters and Numerals
Replace each number with the appropriate Roman numeral and you will obtain the words Lynx, Cedar, Eland, Camel, Llama and Bull. Cedar is the odd one out because the others are animals.

Lewis
Lewis is Lewis Carroll; ML8ML8 sounds like 'I'm late, I'm late' – (the words of the White Rabbit in *Alice's Adventures in Wonderland*). The Rabbit is a Volkswagen car.

Logic 1
B. Each shape moves round once clockwise at each stage. The dot moves two positions. Once the dot has landed in a particular shape, that shape then changes to a new shape in the next diagram.

Logic 2
Q – the position in the alphabet of the letter in the middle is the average of the positions in the alphabet of the four letters surrounding it.

Logic 3
B – first one half of the figure flips around, then the next, and becomes attached to the first available surface of its other half.

Look Alike
52631579 X 29 = 1526315791

Lunch at the Club
40. There must have been an even number of men to receive the answers given.

Mad as a Hatter!
The riddle remained unanswered for many years and even today no one can be sure what, if anything, was the intended solution. Fifteen years after publication, Lewis Carroll, tongue firmly in cheek, made the following whimsical comment.
'Enquiries have been so often addressed to me, as to whether any answer to the Hatter's riddle can be imagined, that I may as well put on record here what seems to me to be a fairly appropriate answer, viz: "Because it can produce a few notes, that they are very flat; and it is never put with the wrong end in front!" This, however, is merely an afterthought; the riddle, as originally invented has no answer at all.'
However, several other suggestions have been ventured, notably by Sam Loyd who said, in true Carrollian fashion, 'the notes for which they are noted are not noted for being musical notes,' and he then went on to point out that 'Poe wrote on both' (our favorite solution) and that 'bill and tales are among their characteristics'. We will leave it to you, our reader, to choose for yourselves your favorite solution or to propose alternatives of your own.

The Magic 11

A Magic '260'

1	63	62	61	4	59	2	8
56	10	54	53	52	11	15	9
24	47	19	44	45	22	42	17
25	34	35	28	29	38	39	32
40	31	30	36	37	27	26	33
41	18	43	21	20	46	23	48
16	50	14	12	13	51	55	49
57	7	3	5	60	6	58	64

Magic Hexagon

The Magic Nine Square

S	P	O	R	T
P	A	P	E	R
O	P	I	N	E
R	E	N	E	W
T	R	E	W	S

S	T	A	F	F
T	I	L	E	R
A	L	A	T	E
F	E	T	E	S
F	R	E	S	H

Magic Square 1

13	8	12	1
2	11	7	14
3	10	6	15
16	5	9	4

Magic Square 2

23	6	19	2	15
10	18	1	14	22
17	5	13	21	9
4	12	25	8	16
11	24	7	20	3

Magic Square 3

24	8	17	1	15
16	5	14	23	7
13	22	6	20	4
10	19	3	12	21
2	11	25	9	18

Magic Square Introduction 1

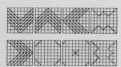

Magic Square Introduction 2

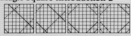

Magic Square Jigsaw Puzzle

92	99	1	8	15	67	74	51	58	40
98	80	7	14	16	73	55	57	64	41
4	81	88	20	22	54	56	63	70	47
85	87	19	21	3	60	62	69	71	28
86	93	25	2	9	61	68	75	52	34
17	24	76	83	90	42	49	26	33	65
23	5	82	89	91	48	30	32	39	66
79	6	13	95	97	29	31	38	45	72
10	12	94	96	78	35	37	44	46	53
11	18	100	77	84	36	43	50	27	59

Magic Squares 1

1.

8	1	6
3	5	7
4	9	2

2.

16	6	11	1
9	3	14	8
2	12	5	15
7	13	4	10

3.

23	4	10	11	17
6	12	18	24	5
9	25	1	7	13
2	8	14	20	21
15	16	22	3	9

4.

24	19	26	6	1	35
25	23	21	7	32	3
20	27	22	2	9	31
15	10	17	33	28	8
16	14	12	34	5	30
11	18	13	29	36	4

5.

4	9	8	47	48	49	10
38	19	20	17	34	35	12
39	37	26	27	22	13	11
43	36	21	25	29	14	7
6	18	28	23	24	32	44
5	15	30	33	16	31	45
40	41	42	3	2	1	46

Magic Squares 2

H	A	R	S	H		M	A	N	S	E
A	B	A	T	E		A	G	A	I	N
R	A	P	I	D		N	A	K	E	D
S	T	I	N	G		S	I	E	V	E
H	E	D	G	E	A	G	L	E	N	D	E	D

(centre)

A	S	I	A	N
G	I	A	N	T
L	A	N	C	E

S	T	O	R	E	E	N	T	E	R	O	A	S	T
T	U	D	O	R				O	R	D	E	R	
O	D	O	U	R				A	D	O	R	E	
R	O	U	G	E				S	E	R	V	E	
E	R	R	E	D				T	R	E	E	S	

Magic Word Square

P	A	P	E	R
A	L	I	V	E
P	I	P	E	S
E	V	E	N	T
R	E	S	T	S

Manhattan

To solve this problem, treat the avenues and streets separately. If everyone lived on the same street, the avenues would look like this:

Number 7, the middle one, would be quickest. If they all lived on the same avenue, then the streets would look like this:

Number 8, the middle one, would be quickest. Therefore, they would meet on avenue 7, street 8.

Married Couples

Janice = Peter, Susan = Alec, Helen = James

Matchsticks

NINE

Mathematicians

Their ages were: 1 – 38; 2 – 39; 3 – 68; 4 – 29; 5 – 26; 6 – 61

Mighty Brainbenders Introduction

I always avoid a kangaroo.

Missing Number 1

494209

The sequence comprises the squares of successive Kaprekar numbers. A Kaprekar number is one which, when it is squared and when the result is divided into two sets of digits – one to the left and one to the right – produces numbers which can then be added to give the original square root. The first few Kaprekar numbers are: 1, 45, 55, 99, 297, 703, 999, etc. For example:

$9^2 = 81$ $8 + 1 = 9$
$55^2 = 3025$ $30 + 25 = 55$
$297^2 = 88209$ $88 + 209 = 297$
703^2 494209 $494 + 209 = 703$

Missing Number 2

2 – the numbers in the first two horizontal and vertical lines, divided by either 5 or 4, give the figure in the final column or row. For example, $15 + 5 = 3$, $8 - 4 = 2$, $3 + 2 = 5$.

Missing Square

G – it is a magic square in which each horizontal, vertical, and corner-to-corner line totals 15 and each number, from 1 to 9, is represented. Black circles are worth 2, and white circles are worth 1.

Missing Sum

The sum consists of the unused segments when displaying the numbers of a seven-segment LED display: that is,

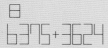

Mr Etcher

Call the artists D, E, M and S, and their vocations d, e, m and s. Then S must be d or m.

1. If S = d, M = s or e; but if M = s, d is the name-sake of M's vocation. So we have: S=d, M=e, E=s and D=m; for if E=m, the namesake of E's vocation is e.

2. If S = d, M = d; for if M = e, E = d (impossible), and if M = s, E = d and D = e (impossible). So we have: S = m, M = d, E = s and D = e. Therefore, collating (1) and (2), Mr. Etcher is the sculptor.

Much Giggling

Denote the names and occupations by letters (the names in capitals, the occupations in lower case) as follows: Baker A, a; Brewer B, b; Butcher C, c; Carter D, d; Draper E, e; Ironmonger F, f; Painter G, g; Saddler H, h; and Smith K, k.

Then, (1) h is the father-in-law off, and K has a married daughter. (2) H is engaged to g's daughter, who has rejected e and a, and D has an unmarried daughter. Therefore, as only two councillors have daughters, (3) K is h and D is g. Again, (4) E is a bachelor and is not e. (5) e's father is brother of Mrs A. (6) b and d are married to each other's sisters; hence (7) A cannot be b or d.

Again we are given two relationships of the form: (8) $\begin{bmatrix} DGX \\ gxb \end{bmatrix}$ and (9) $\begin{bmatrix} KHY \\ gxb \end{bmatrix}$ where x and y are unknown

We also know that A is married; H and E are bachelors f, b, d are married; a and e are bachelors; therefore H may be a, e, C or k. He cannot be e or k; he is therefore c. It follows in (9) that C is d.

Again b may be B, F or G; in (7) he cannot be A. But by (8) he cannot be B or G, and must therefore be F. It follows that G is f. We are only left with A, B and E, who must be a, e and k. Therefore, as A is married, he must be k, and hence by (4) Eisa it follows that B is e. Thus

Mr Baker is the smith
Mr Brewer is the draper
Mr Butcher is the carter
Mr Carter is the painter
Mr Draper is the baker
Mr Ironmonger is the brewer
Mr Painter is the ironmonger
Mr Saddler is the butcher
Mr Smith is the saddler.

Names Riddle

Len. The letters of his name are contained in his relationship to me, uncle, as was the case with the other relatives mentioned.

Napoleon's Problem

1. Choose any point, A, on the circle, and with radius 0-A and centers A, B and C, mark B, C and D. With radius A-C and centers A and D, draw arcs intersecting at E. With radius 0-E and center A, draw the arc cutting the circle at F and G. A, F, D and G are the required points defining the arcs, being the corners of an inscribed square. Although this is elegantly done with six arcs, a five-arc solution is also possible.

2. Assume a unit radius – i.e., O-D= 1
AB = BC = CD,

$$\text{therefore, } <COD = 60°$$
$$\text{therefore, } CD = OD = 1$$
$$<ACD = 90°$$
$$\text{therefore, } AC = \sqrt{3} = AE$$
$$<AOE = 90°$$
$$\text{therefore, } OE = \sqrt{2} = AF$$
$$\text{similarly, } FD = \sqrt{2} \text{ and } <AFD = 90°$$
$$\text{similarly, } AG = GD = v2 \text{ and } <AGD = 90°$$

Nine Green Bottles

1. 24 bottles   2. 20 bottles

Nine-Letter Words

Limousine -the others contain numbers: teleph(one), fr(eight)er and drif(two)od.

Nine Trees 1

Nine Trees 2

No Neighbors

a. Perpendicular
b. Reservation
c. Architecture

Nonsense Sentences

3 – in the others each word is an anagram of a capital city – Rome, Oslo, Lagos; Malé, Manila, Paris; La Paz, Lima, Seoul.

No-Repeat Letters
Trampoline

Number Sequence
1. 111 – these are numbers that, when written, appear the same when viewed upside down.
2. 55 – these are numbers that appear the same when viewed upside down on a calculator.

Numbers 1
117649 (this is a list of cube numbers where either the final digit or the final two digits is their cube root: for example, 513 = 132651)

Numbers 2
The base is 9. Natives 1 and 2 told the truth; natives 3 and 4 told lies.

Numbers Introduction of Intelligence Challengers
381654729

Numbers Introduction of Mind Bafflers

Nursery Rhyme Crossword 1

Nursery Rhyme Crossword 2
Across: Referee (in charge of a football match), Dropped (fallen out), Noisier (sounds louder), Sisters (twin girls)
Down: Rodents (mice), Florins (silver pieces), Reptile (snake), Endures (puts up with)

Nursery Rhyme Crossword 3

Nursery Rhyme Crossword 4

Odd Number
More than 50 percent.

Odd One Out
Thread. The rest are all headless birds: (R)ail, (K)not, (C)row, (F)inch, (P)lover.

Odd One Out 2
C. The others are identical pairs, except that they have been rotated.

Odd One Out 3
C – the others, cut in half vertically, all form words – i.e., elf, cell and fleece – as do their mirror images.

Odd One Out 4
E – A is the same as F; B is the same as C; D is the same as G.

Odd One Out Introduction of Mind Bafflers
The triangle containing the letter A is the odd one out. In all the others the number of sides of the figure coincides with the position in the alphabet of the letter within it.

One Hundred
$96 + \frac{2148}{537}$; $96 + \frac{1752}{438}$; $96 + \frac{1428}{357}$; $94 + \frac{1578}{263}$; $91 + \frac{7524}{836}$;

$91 + \frac{5742}{638}$; $82 + \frac{3456}{187}$; $81 + \frac{7524}{396}$; $81 + \frac{5643}{297}$; $3 + \frac{69258}{714}$

Pair Words

Solution 1	Solution 2
Orange -Lemon	Orange -Seville
Toreador – Seville	Toreador – Matador
Bull – Matador	Bull – Ring
Diamond – Ring	Diamond – Wedding
Nuptials – Wedding	Nuptials – Nubile
Maiden – Nubile	Maiden – Horse*
Sea – Horse	Sea – Swordfish
Sole – Swordfish	Sole – Lemon

* Horses which have not won a race are called maidens.

Palindromic Years
The last time was between the years 999 and 1001, a gap of just two years. The next occasion will be in approximately 8000 years, in the years 9999 and 10001.

Pantechnicon
The driver's reasoning was incorrect. If the birds had flown upwards at an accelerated speed the overall weight would have decreased. If the birds had flown downward or fallen in free fall the weight would have increased. As the birds would have flown at random these two effects would have cancelled each other out and the overall weight would have remained the same.

Pathway
Kangaroos, Kibbutz, Kinkajou, Kibitzer, Kaolin, Kingfisher, Kettles

Peaks

Peoples
Belgian and Bengali are anagrams.

The Polybius Cipher

Read the numbers down and across to find the number in each letter – e.g., H = 23. 'The world great men have not commonly been great scholars, nor its great scholars great men.'
Oliver Wendell Holmes

Probability

1. $^{20}/_{50} \times {}^{30}/_{49} = {}^{600}/_{2450} = 1850$ to 600
2. $^{30}/_{50} \times {}^{20}/_{49} = {}^{600}/_{2450} = 1850$ to 600
3. $^{30}/_{50} \times {}^{19}/_{49} = {}^{380}/_{2450} = 2070$ to 380
4. $^{30}/_{50} \times {}^{29}/_{49} = {}^{870}/_{2450} = 1580$ to 870

P.T. Barnum's Trick Mules

Pyramid

A, AT, ATE, RATE, TREAT, RATTLE, STARLET (STARTLE), SLATTERN, TRANSLATE
Variations may be possible on the smaller words.

Pyramids

1. Anaesthetically; 2. Superficialness

Pyramid Quotation

carnation, hesitant, violent, silken, fugue, wise, wig, my, I

Pyramid Word

L, in, met, rust, saint – instrumentalist

Quotation

'Prosperity is not without many fears and distastes; and adversity is not without comforts and hopes.'
Francis Bacon

Quotation Pyramid

I, It, Fit, Wend, Motet, Tattoo, Shunned, Lethargy, Casserole

Random Numbers

3.3
Difference

0-0	0	1-0	1	2-0	2	3-0	3	4-0	4	5-0	5
0-1	1	1-1	0	2-1	1	3-1	2	4-1	3	5-1	4
0-2	2	1-2	1	2-2	0	3-2	1	4-2	2	5-2	3
0-3	3	1-3	2	2-3	1	3-3	0	4-3	1	5-3	2
0-4	4	1-4	3	2-4	2	3-4	1	4-4	0	5-4	1
0-5	5	1-5	4	2-5	3	3-5	2	4-5	1	5-5	0
0-6	6	1-6	5	2-6	4	3-6	3	4-6	2	5-6	1
0-7	7	1-7	6	2-7	5	3-7	4	4-7	3	5-7	2
0-8	8	1-8	7	2-8	6	3-8	5	4-8	4	5-8	3
0-9	9	1-9	8	2-9	7	3-9	6	4-9	5	5-9	4
	45		37		31		27		25		25

6-0	6	7-0	7	8-0	8	9-0	9		45
6-1	5	7-1	6	8-1	7	9-1	8		37
6-2	4	7-2	5	8-2	6	9-2	7		31
6-3	3	7-3	4	8-3	5	9-3	6		27
6-4	2	7-4	3	8-4	4	9-4	5		25
6-5	1	7-5	2	8-5	3	9-5	4		25
6-6	0	7-6	1	8-6	2	9-6	3		27
6-7	1	7-7	0	8-7	1	9-7	2		31
6-8	2	7-8	1	8-8	0	9-8	1		37
6-9	3	7-9	2	8-9	1	9-9	0		45
	27		31		37		45		330

$^{330}/_{100} = 3.3$

Rebuses 1

1. A little more than kin a little less than kind.
2. Tennis.
3. High IQ.
4. Disorderly conduct.
5. Short measure.
6. Centre of attraction.
7. Rearrangement.
8. Double park.
9. A turn up for the book.
10. Scatterbrain.
11. A snake in the grass.
12. A state of confusion.
13. Cardinal.
14. The Fifth Amendment.
15. Periodic.
16. Short list.
17. All in all.
18. Back street.

Rebuses 2

1. In a spot;
2. A square meal;
3. Sitting tenant;
4. Man about town;
5. Breaking loose;
6. Short measure;
7. Disorderly conduct;
8. Split pea;
9. A piece of the action;
10. Royal prerogative;
11. To read between the lines;
12. Index linked;
13. Part and parcel;
14. Long odds;
15. Mixed metaphor;
16. Industrial action;
17. No man is an island;
18. Mixed doubles;
19. Garden center;
20. Backward glance;
21. The ends of the earth

Reverse Anagram

Hydraulics

A Revolutionary Tale

The T is being dropped into the C. Therefore, the rebus represents the Boston Tea Party.

Riddle

Plant

Riddles

1. Manhattan. 2. Dodecahedron (an anagram of no hard decode).

Roll-a-Penny

In order to win, the punter's coin must fall within the shaded area shown in the diagram. If the center of the coin is outside the shaded area, the coin will be covering part of a line and will, therefore, be a loser. Therefore:

Winning area = 1 sq in
Losing area = 3 sq in

The odds should be 3:1 against and should pay out:

Win	6
Money back	2
Total	8

The actual pay out is:
Total number in squares = $\frac{80}{16}$ = 5 pay out
Number of squares = 16
The odds favour the barker 8 :5.

Roll of Cloth

This is similar to the classic question: 'How long does it take a clock to strike 12 if there is a 1 second between strikes?' In that case, the answer is 11 seconds, because the first two strikes take only 1 second. When it comes to the roll of cloth, the answer is not, as some may suppose, 100 x 3 = 300 seconds. This is incorrect because the 100 pieces are obtained with 99 cuts, the first two pieces coming with a single cut. The answer is, therefore, 99 x 3 = 297 seconds.

Sam Loyd's Hoop-Snake Puzzle

Schiller's Riddle
The Great Wall of China

Select a Crossword
Across: Careers, Natives, Forgone, Resists Down: Conifer, Retires, Envious, Systems

Sequence
B – each of the five circles containing a pattern moves in its own individual sequence – e.g., the black circle moves two forward, three back, two forward; the circle with the cross moves two back, two forward, two back and so on.

Series 1
494209
The sequence comprises the squares of successive Kaprekar numbers. A Kaprekar number is one which, when it is squared and when the result is divided into two sets of digits – one to the left and one to the right – produces numbers which can then be added to give the original square root. The first few Kaprekar numbers are: 1, 9, 45, 55, 99, 297, 703, 999, etc. For example:

$9^2 = 81$	$8 + 1 = 9$
$55^2 = 3025$	$30 + 25 = 55$
$297^2 = 88209$	$88 + 209 = 297$
$703^2 = 494209$	$494 + 209 = 703$

Series 2
so that when viewed in a mirror the numbers 1, 2, 3, 4, 5 appear in sequence.

Seven Clues
The Seven Dwarfs – Sneezy, Doc, Grumpy, Happy, Sleepy, Bashful and Dopey

Shooting Match
Tabulate the results to equal 71. Only three ways are mathematically possible:
25-20-20-3-2-1
25-20-10-10-5-1
50-10-5-3-2-1
The first row is Victor's.
The third row is Madsen's; he hit the bull's-eye.

Shortbread and Shooting Stars
They are all misnomers – 1. Dresden china is made in Meissen; 2. Shooting stars are meteors; 3. Shortbread is a cake or cookie; 4. Jumping bean is a seed; 5. Lead pencil is of graphite; 6. Bald eagle is not bald; 7. Horned toads are lizards; 8. Firefly is a beetle; 9. Prairie dog is a rodent; 10. Catgut comes from sheep or horses.

Signpost
He stands the signpost up so that the arm indicating the place he has come from is pointing in the right direction. The other arms will then point in the right directions too.

A Simple Equation
Add the equations to give
$10000x + 10000y = 50000$
Divide by 10000 to give
$x + y = 5$
Subtract to give
$3502x - 3502y = 3502$
Divide by 3502 to give
$x - y = 1$
Therefore, $x = 3$, $y = 2$

The Simple Twist
12 inches. Our old friend Pythagoras solves this one: $13^2 = 12^2 + 5^2$.

The Slug in the Well
18 days

The Soldiers' Return
Add the percentages together, which gives 70 + 75 + 85 + 80 = 310 among 100 soldiers. This gives three injuries each and four injuries to 10 soldiers (the remainder when dividing 310 by 100). The last percentage is, therefore, 10.

Something in Common 1
They are all anagrams of American states – Maine, Oklahoma and Utah.

Something in Common 2
They have all different, established and accepted spellings in America: honor, check, theater, license and center. This is the result of nineteenth-century nationalism on the part of Noah Webster, of Webster's Dictionary fame.

Spherical
Pious (sanctimonious); happiness (contentment); exodus (evacuation); riotous (disorderly); impetus (stimulus); confess (divulge); antics (tomfoolery); logistics (coordination)

The Spider and the Fly

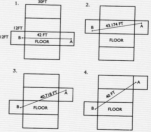

Diagram 4 shows that the shortest route is 40 feet. The spider crawls along five of the six sides of the room.

Spot on the Table
58 inches

The ordinary schoolboy would rightly treat this as a quadratic equation. Here is the actual arithmetic. Double the product of the two distances from the walls. This gives us 144, which is the square of 12. The sum of the two distances is 17. If we add these two numbers, 12 and 17, together and also subtract one from the other, we get the two answers: either 29 or was the radius, which means that the diameter was 8 inches or io inches. A table of the latter dimensions would be absurd, so the former must be correct.

Square

CACOPHONY

Square 2
Laughable

Square Numbers 1
Across: 4489, 1225, 4761, 2809, 3969, 5329, 4225, 3136
Down: 2916, 1156, 6561, 7921, 4624, 5929, 9604, 3249

Square Numbers 2
The lowest square number is 139854276; the highest is 923187456.

The Square of Fibonacci
$1681/144 = (41/42)^2$
$-5 = 961/144 = (31/12)^2$
$+5 = 2401/144 = (49/42)^2$
The answer is not, of course, an integer.

Square of the Sixth Order

1	35	4	33	32	6
30	8	27	28	11	7
24	23	15	16	14	19
13	17	21	22	20	18
12	26	10	9	29	25
31	2	34	3	5	36

The Square Series
Take, for example, the square number 784 (28²). The sum of its digits is 19, which in turn totals 10 and which in turn totals 1. The next square number is 841 (29²). The sum of s digits is 13, and the sum of these digits is 4. Starting from 1, successive square numbers produce the sequence 1, 4, 9, 7, 7, 9, 4, 1, 9, and this series, when worked out this way, will repeat to infinity.

Square Words 1
a. Captivate
b. Juxtapose
c. Kingsized
d. Bystander
e. Turquoise

Square Words 2
Necessary – requisite; calculate – determine; luxuriant – excessive

Squares
a.

b.

Squaring the Urn

Stair-Rods

Lay the stair-rods across the puddle, making sure that they are equal distances apart, measure the length of each stair-rod from top to bottom of the puddle as indicated by the arrows and add the measurements together. Divide the figure so obtained by the number of stair-rods lying across the puddle, and then multiply that figure by the width of the puddle to give the area.

Strike Out

A̶ S̶ H̶ O̶ R̶ T̶ P̶ H̶ R̶ A̶ S̶ E̶

'Swiftly I Come . . .'
A reflection in a mirror.

Symbols

Synchronized Synonyms

Crack (fracture, splinter); Contemplate (meditate, ruminate); August (imposing, majestic); Subterfuge (artifice, pretense); Foreword (preamble, prologue); Childish (juvenile, immature); Viable (feasible, workable); Macabre (dreadful, ghoulish)

Tangrams

Target

C. In the outer circle a dot is added at 90° each time. In the middle circle the number of dots increases by one each time and the first dot moves through 90°, with the additional dots placed at 45° intervals. In the inner circle the number of dots increases by one each time and the first dot moves through 45°, with the additional dots placed at 45° intervals.

Target Crossword

Vulcan, wicket, yeoman, zombie, violin, vapor, twenty, legend, sorrow, sloshy, smooch, sinful, siphon, saucer, pavior, pestle

Tell Me Who

Musicians

Think of a Number

729. To work out the answer, first draw up a table:

Range	Squares	Cube	Both
13-499	16, 25,36, 49, 64, 81, 100, 121, 144, 169, 196, 225, 256,289,324,361, 400, 441,484	27, 64, 125, 216,343	64
500-1300	529, 576, 625, 676, 729, 784,841, 900, 961, 1024, 1089, 1156, 1225, 1296	512, 729, 1000	729

Possible true answers:
1 and 2- no, there are no cubes under 500
1 and 3- no, there are no squares under 500
2 and 3-yes, over 500 there is a square and a cube (729)

Thirteenth-Century Word Search

1. Aimcrier, 2. Bellibone, 3. Bellytimber, 4. Chantpleure, 5. Fellowfeel, 6. Flesh-spades, 7. Keaks, 8. Lubberwort, 9. Merry-go-sorry, 10. Mubbles-fubbles, 11. Murfles, 12. Poplolly, 13. Prick-me-dainty, 14. Smellsmock, 15. Wurps, 16. Tumps

Three Cryptograms

1. 'I'm very well acquainted too with matters mathematical, I understand equations, both the simple and quadratical.' *W.S. Gilbert*
2. 'I remember being handed a score composed by Mozart at the age of eleven. What could I say? I felt like De Kooning who was asked to comment on a certain abstract painting and answered in the negative. He was then told it was the work of a celebrated monkey. "That's different. For a monkey it's terrific".' *Igor Stravinsky*
3. 'He who builds according to every man's advice will have a crooked house.' *Danish Proverb*

Three-Letter Words

Take the first letter of the first word, the second letter of the second word, the third letter of the third word, then the first letter of the fourth word and so on to reveal the message 'more power to your elbow'.

Tiles

Tower of Hanoi Patience

In the example illustrated, the 10 cannot be moved first without breaking the rules. It must be got to the top of a column as soon as possible. The opening moves of the puzzle are 4 under 10, 7 under 9, 5 under 7, 4 under 5 and 10 into the vacancy. You are on your own now, except that we will tell you that the next step is to get the 9 under the 10.

Track Words

a. Misapprehension
b. Knickerbockers

Train

$$\frac{((1.5 + 025) \times 60)}{50}$$
= 21 mins or 2 minutes 6 seconds

Triangles 1

56

Triangles 2

Construct a triangular pyramid.

Triangles 3

The Triangular H

Triple Acrostic

A do	R in	G
M usk	E tee	
B an	D ag	R
E con	O miz	E
R eite	R atio	N

Triplicities

GI = Gemini W = Water

In each segment of the circle are the first and last letters of the astrological signs surrounding the initial letter of their corresponding element.

In astrology the word triplicities is another name for the elements: Fire, Earth, Air and Water.

Twee and Tug

'What hat's that?' said Bill.

'The flat hat,' said Ben.

'Oh, that hat,' said Bill.

'That's that then.

Bill and Ben were a couple of puppet characters, known as the Flowerpot Men, which appeared on a children's program in the early days of British television in the 1950s. Their language closely resembled the 'flop lopy plop' dialogue of the coded text.

Two 5 x 5 Magic Squares

R	U	D	E	R
U	V	U	L	A
D	U	C	A	T
E	L	A	T	E
R	A	T	E	D

S	O	L	I	D
O	P	E	R	A
L	E	G	A	L
I	R	A	T	E
D	A	L	E	S

Two 6 x 6 Magic Squares

B	A	T	T	E	R
A	R	R	I	V	E
T	R	I	P	O	D
T	I	P	P	L	E
E	V	O	L	V	E
R	E	D	E	E	M

E	S	T	A	T	E
S	H	A	V	E	N
T	A	L	E	N	T
A	V	E	R	S	E
T	E	N	S	E	R
E	N	T	E	R	S

The Ultimate Counterfeit Coin Puzzle

The three operations are first to weigh coins 1, 2, 3 and 4 against 5, 6, 7 and 8; and then to weigh coins 9, 10, 11 and 4 against 1, 2, 3 and 8. There are now five possible actions.

1. If the scales were balanced both times, 12 is the counterfeit coin. Weigh it against another to see if it is heavy or light.

2. If the scales were balanced in the first weighing but not in the second, weigh coin 9 against coin 10 to see which way as in the second weighing. If they balance, 11 is the counterfeit and will be heavy or light as shown by the second weighing.

3. If the scales were balanced in the second weighing but not in the first, weigh coin 5 and against coin 6 to see which tips in the same way as in the first weighing. If they balance, 7 is the counterfeit and will be heavy or light as shown by the first weighing.

4. If the scales were off-balance the same way both times, weigh coin 4 against another coin. If they balance, the counterfeit is 8 and will be heavy or light as shown by the first two weighings.

5. If the scales were off-balance in opposite ways in the first two weighings, weigh coin 1 against coin 2 to see which tips in the second weighing. If they balance, 3 is the counterfeit coin and would be heavy or light as shown in the second weighing.

The Ultimate Shunting Puzzle

Train to 15-meter siding; collect coach B. Back to 15-meter siding; . leave B in 5-meter siding. Back to 15-meter siding; up to top; pick up A and push down on to B in 5-meter siding. Reverse up to top. Drop B in its original place and come back with A to the top. Take A to 5-meter siding and leave. Reverse up to top; collect B and reverse to top. Leave B in A's original position. Reverse train and go across to 15-meter siding. Push A up to B's original position and return train to starting point.

Unique Number

It contains the numbers i to 9 in alphabetical order.

The Urban Riddle

Four towns can be found, one on each line: Rome, Ely, Paris, Chester.

The Village Simpleton

Sunday

Virgil's Riddle

At the bottom of a well

Visual Deceptions

1. They are both the same. 2. B. 3. A

The Water Butt

He tilted the butt until the water came up to the top edge without any running over. As the level of the water did not reach point X, the butt was not half-full. If it had reached point X, it would have been exactly half-full; but if point X had been submerged, it would have been more than half-full.

Water to Wine

As water is slightly heavier than wine, if you remove the bung, remove the bottle cap, upend the full bottle of water over the bung hole and make a good seal, the water will be exchanged for wine.

What the Dickens!

Martin Chuzzlewit, Nicholas Nickleby, The Old Curiosity Shop, David Copperfield, Barnaby Rudge, Great Expectations, A Tale of Two Cities, Oliver Twist, Dombey and Son, Hard Times

What's the Connection

Each has an anagram partner on the same theme - lemon (fruit); Kyoto (Japanese city); Arnold (man's name).

What's the Link
They are all books of the Bible – 1. Exodus; 2. Numbers; 3. Judges; 4. Ruth; 5. Kings; 6. Chronicles; 7. Job; 8. Proverbs; 9. Mark; 10. Revelation

Where There is a Will There is a Way
There were only three beneficiaries – son, father and grandfather.

Who's Who
They all bear people's names, either factual or fictional: 1. Mickey Finn; 2. Walter Mitty; 3. Hobson's choice; 4. Sally Lunn; 5. Davy Jones's locker; 6. Beau Brummell; 7. Sam Browne; 8. Tony; 9. Molotov cocktail; 10. Darby and Joan

The Wolf, Goat and Cabbage
The steps are as follows, with W = wolf, G = goat and C = cabbage:
1. Man takes G to other bank and returns to collect C.
2. Man takes C to other bank and returns with G.
3. Man leaves G and takes W to other bank, where he leaves W with C.
4. Man returns to collect G.

Word Circle
Enrage, Geisha, Haggle, Legato, Topple, Legion, Onrush, Shaken

Word Construction 1
Categorize, Feathered, Woebegone, Together, Attendance, Fatherless, Inhabitant, Malefactor, Redevelop, Damageable

Word Construction 2
Barbecue, infantry, fatherland, discourage, artifice, outwardbound, soupkitchen, pollinate, meadowland, beleaguered

Word Play Introduction of Brain Puzzlers
Its now seen live	(James I. Rambo)
Flit on cheering angel	(Lewis Carroll)
Govern, clever lad	(Dmitiri Borgmann)
The door ring tided ill	
Kill bleaters, ah! tough meat	(Carter/Russell)
Best in prayer	
Sign long wedded	
Hearts go to man's aid	(Loris B. Curtis)
One fire went right on	(Jeane E. Roman)

Word Play Introduction of Intelligence Challengers
1. Cleave
2. Sequoia
3. Triennially (Tinily and Renal)
4. Nominates (Minnesota)
5. Manufacture (also, of course, Manufactured, Manufacturer/s, Manufacturing)
6. Queueing
7. Best, Worst
8. Typewriter

Word Power
1. Deciduous 2. Earthworm 3. Hyperbole 4. Magnitude 5. Recumbent 6. Witticism 7. Hidebound 8. Liquorice 9. Loincloth

Word Search
The positive word form as in the grid is given first; the better known, negative form is given in brackets.
1. Advertent (inadvertent);
2. Infectant (disinfectant);
3. Histamine (antihistamine);
4. Corrigible (incorrigible);
5. Evitable (inevitable);
6. Odorant (deodorant);
7. Consolate (disconsolate);
8. Wieldy (unwieldy);
9. Canny (uncanny);
10. Biotic (antibiotic);
11. Couth (uncouth);
12. Effable (ineffable);
13. Kempt (unkempt);
14. Licit (illicit);
15. Furl (unfurl)

Word Square
When you successfully complete this puzzle you will have proved beyond doubt qualities of determination and patience.

Words
Taking A = 1, B = 2, C = 3 and so on, the sum of the letters in each word totals 100, as do the letters in Socrates and Robin Hood.

Words 2
The 14-letter words are:
1. Administration,
2. Extinguishable,
3. Correspondence,
4. Misappropriate,
5. Predeterminate.
The 15-letter words are:
1. Cinematographer,
2. Psychotherapist,
3. Experimentation,
4. Comprehensively,
5. Totalitarianism

Work It Out
Making a mountain out of a molehill.

Wot! No Vowels
Pyx, Myrrh, Why, Sylph, Syzygy, Rhythm, Lymph, Sly, Shyly, Shy, Slyly, Spy, Try, Ply

Wynne's Winner
Across: 2. Log 4. Aisle 6. Pensive 8. Boot 9. Belt 11. Darn 12. Need 14. Fort 15. Grip 16. Toil 18. Rasp 19. Noel 21. Dine 22. Nearest 24. Knock 25. Elk
Down: 1. Moss 2. Lint 3. Glib 4. Aeon . Even 6. Portion 7. Elegant 8. Baron so. Terse 11. Dot 13. Dip 17. Leek 18. Risk 20. Lane 2!. Deck 23. Roll

Zoetrope
Three-letter: FOB – IRE
Four-letter: CROP – FURS
Five-letter: COBRA – FREUD